CorelD

PRISMA Computer Courses are structured, practical guides to mastering the most popular computer programs.
PRISMA books are course books, giving step-by-step instructions, which take the user through basic skills to advanced functions in easy to follow, manageable stages.

Now available:

dBase IV
Excel 4.0 for Windows
Lotus 1-2-3
Lotus 1-2-3 for Windows
Microsoft Office
MS-DOS 3.3 to 5.0
MS-DOS 6.2
Norton Desktop for Windows
Novell Netware
UNIX
Windows
WordPerfect 6.0
WordPerfect for Windows
Visual Basic for Windows
Word 6.0 for Windows
Norton Desktop for Windows

Michael Monka
Werner Voß

CorelDRAW! 5

PRISMA COMPUTER COURSE

Prisma Computer Courses first published in Great Britain 1992 by

Het Spectrum
PO Box 2996
London N5 2TA

Translation: George Hall
Production: LINE UP text productions

© 1995 Uitgeverij Het Spectrum BV, Utrecht

For the English translation
© 1995 Uitgeverij Het Spectrum BV, Utrecht

ISBN   1 85365 396 9

British Library Cataloguing-in-Publication Data.
A catalogue record for this book is available from the British Library.

Contents

Foreword

CorelDRAW! is one of the most extensive programs for processing graphic data. Until recently, this kind of advanced graphic program was almost exclusively used by specialists. However, the price of PCs and professional software has now decreased so dramatically that applications developed to compile and display large-scale graphical work and presentations have come into the reach of the everyday user.

There is also another aspect which has facilitated this process. The demand for information has multiplied in both private and professional circles, while time to read concentrated documentation seems to be at a minimum. Accordingly, under the motto *a picture says more than a thousand words*, ever increasing use of visual information and graphic presentation is being made.

In order to create explicit visual information, graphic programs must satisfy certain criteria. They must be easy to operate, provide many graphical resources and assistance and be able to combine text and tables. In addition, it is also important that the user is able to get to grips with the program quickly and easily. CorelDRAW! is able to fulfil all these conditions.

A graphic program should be able to compile images in various ways. Just as grammar and style play a role in text, comparable (structural) elements also play a part in the creation of images. This book also takes these aspects into account. All the important CorelDRAW! techniques are discussed, and tips for graphic display of all components are given. In this way, both beginners and advanced users can obtain satisfaction from working with this program.

The package not only contains the CorelDRAW! program but also a number of other applications, including the desktop publishing program CorelVENTURA. All these programs are discussed in detail in this book. Practical examples illustrate how to combine text and images in an attractive way.

This book is written in such a way that you do need to work through it right from the beginning to the very end. At the beginning of each new chapter, there is a brief outline of the program functions that are dealt with in that chapter. This is followed by a short list of the chapter contents so that the experienced user can recognise the features at a glance. The diverse program functions are subsequently explained in detail: how to apply them and make effective use of them. Examples are given to indicate the steps required. All examples and tips are clearly and orderly laid out.

This structure enables the reader to study the chapters individually. Any unknown terminology is generally handled in the introduction to the section.

We presume that the CorelDRAW! program, the other Corel programs and the Windows interface have been installed on your computer. In addition, we expect you to know the basic skills of working with Windows: how to open and close Window applications and how to use the mouse. If this is not the case, we advise you to read Appendices A and B first.

Finally, we wish to indicate that the first chapter, to a certain degree, occupies an exceptional position in this book. The basic principles and most important operating features are explained here, along with a complete introductory overview. This theory is elaborated in the course of the book. Accordingly, it is possible to gain attractive results within a very short time.

1 CorelDRAW! Introduction

This chapter deals with all facets of the CorelDRAW! window: the window frame, menubars, toolbox and colour palette. In addition, the operation of CorelDRAW! in the various program components is outlined.

The topics in this chapter:

- starting up and closing down CorelDRAW!
- the user interface and screen components such as the window frame, title bar, menubar, scroll bars, status line, Ruler and colour palette
- work area (drawing area for graphic objects)
- print preview
- drawing tools in the toolbox (rectangle, lines, ellipses, text, zoom etc.)
- operation of the menus and dialog windows.

1.1 Starting up CorelDRAW!

The ease of operation of a program depends to a large extent on the facilities provided by the work environment. CorelDRAW! works with the Windows interface and can only be implemented in combination with Windows. Because Windows has a certain standard method of operation, all programs which run under Windows are operated in a similar way. For instance, starting up programs always takes place in exactly the same way.

As mentioned in the Foreword, we presume that Corel-DRAW! is already installed on your computer. If that is not the case, you should read Appendix A first. You will need to start up Windows prior to starting up Corel-

DRAW! Therefore, behind the DOS prompt (C:\>), type

```
win
```

In Windows, the various programs are gathered into program groups which are collectively managed by the Program Manager. If you have installed CorelDRAW! as described in Appendix A, the program will be stored in the
Corel5 group which is created during the installation.
This group contains the various components of the program package, each one represented by its own icon.
Open the program group by moving the mouse pointer
to the folder icon with the name CorelDRAW! and then
double click (click twice in rapid succession) on the left
mouse button. Appendices B and E deal with the most
important mouse actions, such as clicking, double clicking and dragging, for example.

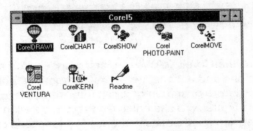

In addition to CorelDRAW!, the CorelVENTURA, Corel-
CHART and CorelSHOW are also stored in this group.
The precise contents will depend of course on what you
have installed. All these programs will be discussed in
this book. The CorelDRAW! program is started up by
placing the mouse pointer on the appropriate icon and
double clicking. The CorelDRAW! opening screen appears.

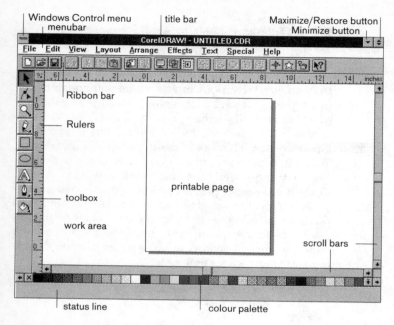

This is the CorelDRAW! user and work environment. All functions and actions are operated from this point. The most important screen components are displayed in the above figure. We shall discuss them in detail in the following sections. Because the various functions are easier to comprehend when they are being applied, we shall begin by creating several simple images.

1.2   The CorelDRAW! user interface

The CorelDRAW! work environment has many important functions for operation and display. Many of these can be (partly) activated or deactivated to produce the greatest possible overview and ease of operation. The title bar at the top of the screen shows the program and the file name.

Windows Control menu   current filename   Maximize/Restore button

Minimize button

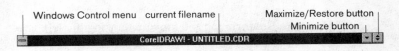

As long as the file has not yet been saved, it has the standard name UNTITLED.CDR. The menubar is situated under the title bar:

menubar with the names of the menus

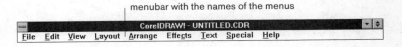

Place the mouse pointer on one of the menu names and click once. The corresponding menu is opened:

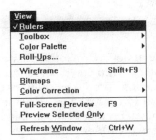

A menu contains commands and options for working with graphic objects or managing graphic files, such as saving or printing a drawing. The status bar is situated under the Ribbon bar or at the bottom of the screen. You can place it at the top or the bottom as required by opening the *Special* menu, clicking on *Preferences*, activating the View tabsheet and clicking on the required option. The status line indicates the position and size of graphic objects.

status line

There are Rulers along the top and flanking the left side of the working area to show the size of the object. You can activate or deactivate these Rulers as required.

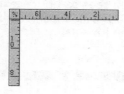

The colour palette is situated at the bottom of the screen. This enables you to quickly select a colour for a specified graphic object.

The Ribbon bar, a new function in CorelDRAW!, is displayed under the menu bar. You can change the Ribbon bar to suit your own needs. The icons (buttons) on the Ribbon bar enable you to activate the commonly-used functions. When you click on one of these buttons, the relevant function is immediately executed. If you wish to know which button represents which function, move the mouse pointer to it without clicking. The name of the button appears in a small yellow box next to the mouse pointer. The status line then also gives a brief description of the feature.

The toolbox (see the opposite page) is displayed as a box flanking the left-hand side of the screen. All the important drawing instruments are included here.

The Pick tool (arrow) has the same function as the cursor in a word processor. Under this is the Shape tool

which is used to change the shape of an object. The Zoom tool enables you to enlarge or reduce various parts of the work area. The Freehand tool draws lines and curves. The Rectangle and El-lipse tools enable you to draw these shapes per-fectly. The letter A in the toolbox represents the Artistic Text tool with which you can type text in an image. The Outline and Fill tools enable you to modify respectively the outlines and surfaces of graphic objects.

If you click on a tool with a small triangle in the lower right-hand corner and hold the mouse button down a lit-tle longer, a so-called *flyout* menu appears, providing ex-tra tools belonging to the same category. If you wish to obtain quick help about a tool or button while you are drawing, click using the **right** mouse button on the tool or button. A help text then appears with concise informa-tion and a summary of the most important application possibilities.

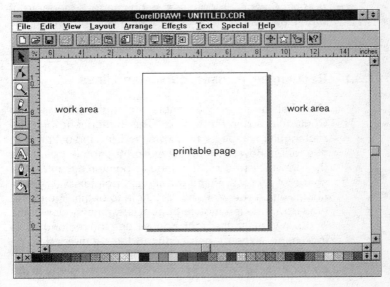

The actual working area is the drawing window and occupies the greater part of the screen. The graphic objects can be created and moved around in this area. The size of the drawing window itself can be altered. The printable page is displayed in the drawing window. When the program has been installed, the printable page is geared to letter-size (A4) drawings. The page borders are shown; all drawn objects within the edges of the page will be printed on paper. In chapter 2, we shall apply settings which will apply to all created images.

It is, of course, possible to draw graphic objects outside the printable page. You can store them there or use that area as a practice area.

1.3   The drawing tools

The operational method for creating drawings remains the same, regardless of the size and complexity of the graphic objects. In principle, each image is made up of the same basic elements such as lines and rectangles etc.

1.3.1   Rectangles, ellipses, curves and lines

We shall begin with a simple rectangle. Click on the Rectangle box in the toolbox. The 'button' showing the rectangular shape is now 'pressed in', indicating that this tool is now active. Now move the mouse pointer to the drawing window; the mouse pointer assumes the shape of a cross. Place the mouse pointer at the position at which you wish the rectangle to begin. Press and hold down the left mouse button. Drag the mouse pointer downwards to the right. You will see the rectangle taking shape. When it has acquired the required size, release the mouse button. Now fill the rectangle with colour by clicking on a colour in the colour palette at the bottom of the screen. If you click on the desired colour with the right mouse button, the outline of the object is given that colour.

Draw another rectangle in the same way, so that the screen looks something like this:

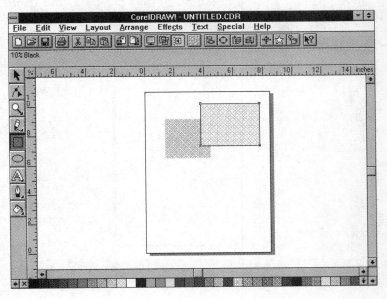

Prior to trying out the other tools in a similar way, we shall give a short description of another CorelDRAW! concept: the wire model. Each graphic object is displayed just as it will come out of the printer. If you only wish to see the graphic object as a wire model, in other words, the basic structure without colour, select the *Wireframe* option from the *View* menu, or press the shortcut key combination Shift+F9.

As mentioned, the objects appear on the screen in the same way as they will come out of the printer, thus with colour, shading and patterns. A newly-drawn object is automatically added. But as objects become larger and more complex, you will see that the time taken to construct or redraw the screen becomes longer. If you wish to work more quickly, it is advisable to work in the Wireframe View.

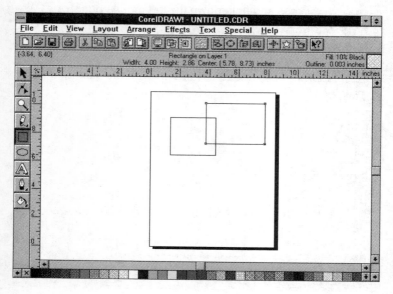

You can also apply a different setting to view the graphic objects. You can activate the Full-Screen Preview mode by selecting this option from the *View* menu or by clicking on the Full-Screen Preview button; you can also press the shortcut key F9. However, you can only view the drawing in this mode, you cannot edit it. The printable page is shown on the entire screen. Press F9 once again to return to the original situation. If you then wish to work further in the Wireframe View, press Shift+F9. This is advisable when you wish to implement various screen activities such as moving and enlarging the drawing window.

You also have the Ellipse tool and the Freehand tool. A circle or ellipse is drawn as follows:

1) Click once on the Ellipse tool.
2) Move the mouse pointer to an empty space on the screen.
3) Press and hold down the left mouse button.
4) Drag the mouse pointer in the required direction.
5) Release the mouse button.

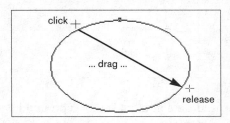

The status line displays several pieces of information. These data always refer to the last drawn or selected object. In our last example, the status line would indicate that we are drawing an ellipse with a certain width and height. At the right-hand side of the status line, there are data about outline and colour (if any).

Click on one of the colours in the colour palette at the bottom of the screen. The data on the status bar change. Try this in all the following examples, switching off the Wireframe View so that you can check the result. The colours you wish to use should be visible in their respective areas.

We shall now draw a curve. The procedure closely resembles that used to draw other figures:

1) Click on the Freehand tool so that the button appears to be pressed down.

2) Place the mouse pointer where the curve is to begin.
3) Press and hold down the left mouse button.
4) Draw a random curve on the screen.
5) Release the mouse button when you have finished.

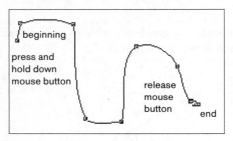

If you wish to draw a straight line, you proceed in almost exactly the same way, only you do not hold down the mouse button. Click on the position where the line is to begin and click. Move the mouse pointer to the position where the line is to end and click again.

1.3.2 Text

In CorelDRAW!, texts are regarded as being graphic objects. This has the advantage that they can be altered separately. In this way, it is possible to create your own fonts. Proceed as follows to add a text to a drawing:

1) Activate the Artistic Text tool; the button appears to be pressed down.
2) Place the cursor at the position where the text is to begin.
3) Click on the left mouse button.

The so-called *text cursor* then appears. Type the text **Welcome to CorelDRAW!**. The screen will now look like this (we have used the Zoom tool to make the figure more legible):

text cursor

It is very easy to change text attributes in CorelDRAW!. When you press the Ctrl+F2 key combination, a roll-up *Text* menu appears on the screen. This is a kind of flexible dialog window, providing various facilities for editing the text. You can place this roll-up menu anywhere on the screen by clicking on its title bar and dragging it to the required position.

By clicking on one of the buttons in the middle of the window, you can determine the text alignment: right, left or centred. Click on the required button and then on the *Apply* button to apply the settings to the selected text.

The size of the text (the default setting is 24 points) can be altered by clicking on one of the arrows to the right of the text box or by changing the value in the text box directly. The font size is normally measured in points (roughly 72 to an inch), but you can also specify the size in *inches, picas, millimeters, ciceros* or *didots*. You can choose a font from the many possibilities offered in the list at the top of the window. The AvantGarde font is the default setting unless you have installed no TrueType fonts during the installation procedure.

You select a font by clicking on the arrow next to the text box. A drop-down list appears. Click on the required font in the list. If you cannot see all the fonts listed, click on the scroll bar at the right of the list to move through the available letter types.

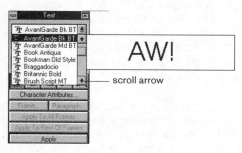

scroll arrow

In addition, the *Text* roll-up menu enables you to apply various attributes to the font. If you want to change the way text is displayed, you have to select the text first, unless you activate the roll-up menu immediately before typing the text. To select the text, click on the Pick tool and then on the text.

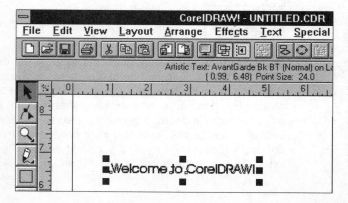

Make the following alterations in the roll-up menu and click on the *Apply* button:

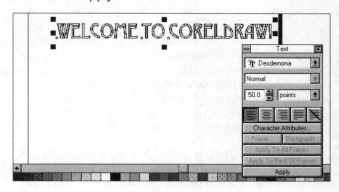

The text is then displayed on the screen in the new style. The status line shows the information referring to the attributes and size of the corresponding text object. The 50 points font size makes the text easily legible. Further on in this book, we shall discuss the CorelDRAW! Zoom function which enables you to enlarge each part of the work area.

Close the *Text* roll-up menu by clicking on the Control menu button in the top left-hand corner of this box.

1.4   Selecting and altering objects

As you would expect, changes can be made to drawn objects, although not all mutations are possible. The changes to which we refer consist of moving a rectangle to another position on the screen, changing an ellipse proportionally, rotating a text etc. To make these modifications, you need to use the Pick tool and the Shape tool.

Pick tool
Shape tool

1.4.1   The Pick tool

You can use the Pick tool to implement the following tasks:

- selecting objects
- moving objects
- stretching and shrinking objects
- making proportional changes to objects
- rotating objects
- skewing (slanting) objects

The Pick tool is in fact the most important tool in Corel-DRAW! and you will probably use it the most. It can be applied in the following ways:

Selecting objects

You have to select an object in order to be able to edit it:

1) Click on the Pick tool.
2) Move the mouse pointer to one of the rectangles we drew previously.
3) Place the mouse pointer on the edge of the rectangle and click once.

The rectangle is activated. Eight small black blocks, the *handles*, appear around the rectangle.

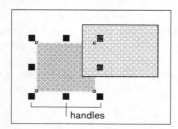

handles

The status line now provides information about the selected rectangle. If you select a different object in the same way, you will see that the information on the status line changes appropriately. Eight handles are always placed around each selected object.

There are two methods of selecting several different objects at the same time. With the first method, proceed as described above, but at step 3, press and hold down the Shift key. Then click on the other objects in question. The screen shows that the entire selection frame becomes larger with each selection.

The second method of selecting several objects at one time involves using the *marquee* option (a blue dotted frame). First click in the free space to undo any previous selections. Then proceed as follows to select several objects at once.

1) Place the mouse pointer in the free space near to the required objects.
2) Press and hold down the left mouse button.
3) Drag the mouse across the objects to be selected. You see a dotted frame enclosing the objects.

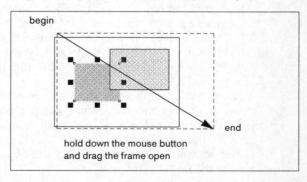

begin

hold down the mouse button
and drag the frame open

end

4) Release the mouse button. The selection frame with the eight blocks appears containing the selected objects.

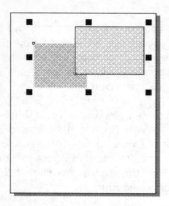

selected rectangles

If you wish to make certain changes, such as applying a new colour or a different line thickness, it is convenient to select the various objects in one go. This can save you quite a lot of time.

Moving objects

You can also move selected objects. This is done as follows:

1) Select the object using the Pick tool and place the mouse pointer on the edge of the selected object.
2) Press and hold down the left mouse button.
3) Move the mouse pointer to a different position on the screen and release the mouse button.

You can move an object to any position on the screen in this way. During the process of moving, the object is replaced by a blue dotted frame which indicates the current position of the object. If you use the right mouse button instead of the left, a copy of the object is left behind at the original position.

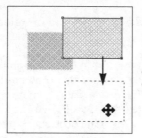

dragging while holding
down the mouse button

The information on the status line changes during the moving process. The distance to the original position is given and the angle of relocation. When the object has been moved, the handles appear once more. These handles have a special significance: you can use them to change the size of the object.

Stretching and shrinking objects

We shall use a rectangle to illustrate how to stretch an object:

1) Click on the Pick tool.
2) Place the mouse pointer on one of the four handles in the middle of one of the sides (thus not on the corners). The mouse pointer assumes the shape of a cross.

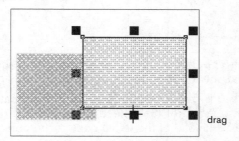

drag

3) Press and hold down the mouse button. Drag the mouse pointer horizontally or vertically to a different

position on the drawing area and release the mouse button.

In this way, it is possible to stretch or shrink an object in any desired direction. Experiment using all kinds of objects to try out the possibilities. You will also notice that it is convenient to define texts in CorelDRAW! as objects. Stretching and shrinking text can produce some rather interesting effects.

Proportional enlargement and reduction

Proportional enlargement and reduction is referred to as *scaling*. Scaling means changing an object's length and width at the same time without changing the ratio between these. The figure below illustrates this:

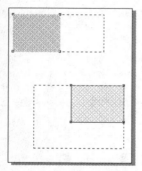

The upper rectangle is enlarged on one side. In contrast, the lower rectangle is enlarged proportionally; the original mutual proportions are retained. Select one of the rectangles you drew previously for use in the following example:

1) Place the mouse pointer on one of the four corner handles of the rectangle. The mouse pointer as-

sumes the shape of a cross.

2) Press and hold down the left mouse button. Drag the mouse pointer towards the middle of the rectangle.

3) Release the mouse button.

The current sizes of the sides of the rectangle have changed, but the proportions have remained the same.

Rotating and skewing objects

If you wish to rotate or skew (slant) objects, double click on the outline of the object. The familiar handles change into small arrows.

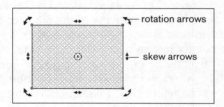

If you select and move the corner arrows, the object is rotated. To illustrate this, we shall rotate an existing text. Proceed as follows:

1) Click on the Pick tool to select the text. Handles appear around the text.

2) Click on the outline of the text. (You could also have double clicked on the text in one go.)

3) Place the mouse pointer on one of the rounded arrows in one of the corners. The mouse pointer changes into a cross.

4) Press and hold down the left mouse button. Drag the frame until the text has acquired the desired angle of rotation.

5) Release the mouse button.

The text will now look something like this:

If you wish to skew (slant) a text, proceed as described in steps 1 to 3 above. Then place the mouse pointer on one of the straight arrows on one of the sides of the object. Press and hold down the mouse button, and drag the mouse pointer in one of the directions indicated by the arrow. The slope of the object changes. Release the mouse button when the skewing has reached the required angle. The figure below illustrates the type of result you can gain by skewing a text:

1.4.2   The Shape tool

The Shape tool provides almost infinite possibilities for altering the shape of objects. The figures opposite displays a possibility of distorting the text:

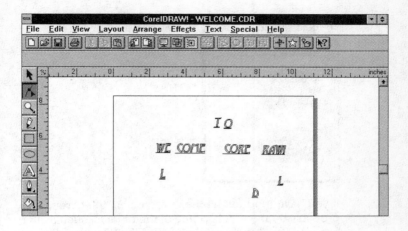

As a simple example, we shall take a rectangle and round off the corners. Create a rectangle first if necessary, and then proceed as follows:

1) Click on the Shape tool in the toolbox.

2) The mouse pointer changes from a cross into a triangular arrow.
3) Select the rectangle by clicking on it. The so-called *nodes* appear on the four sides.
4) Click on one of these nodes and drag the mouse pointer along the outline of the rectangle to round it off.
5) When the corners have been sufficiently rounded, release the mouse button.

In this way, you can round a rectangle progressively.
Various kinds of reshaping and deformation using the nodes can be applied to selected objects. This applies to all kinds of objects including text which has been defined as an object.

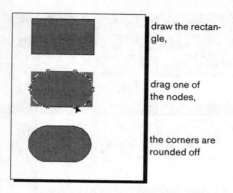

draw the rectangle,

drag one of the nodes,

the corners are rounded off

If you have tried out all these examples, the screen will probably be rather full. Some of the objects, such as the text, may be hardly recognisable. For this reason, we shall now introduce a new tool which enables you to enlarge or reduce the work area progressively.

1.5 The Zoom tool

If you wish to enlarge separate objects or certain parts of graphic objects on the screen, click on the Zoom tool. This is the button in the toolbox which looks like a magnifying glass. A flyout menu opens, providing six icons representing the following functions:

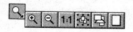

- progressive zoom in
- zoom out (to last chosen level)
- view actual size (one inch on the screen is one inch out of the printer)
- zoom to selected (optimum zoom for selected objects)
- zoom to all objects (all objects, regardless of size, are shown)
- zoom to drawing page.

We shall use the *eye.cdr* file from the *samples* directory as an example. Open the *File* menu and click on *Open*. Select the file from the appropriate directory (you can of course use your own drawing or any other file of your choice).

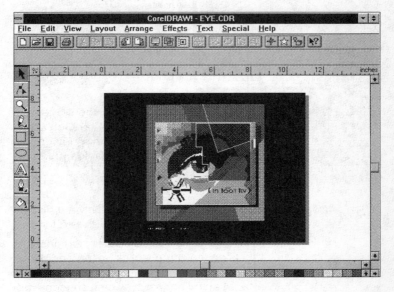

To zoom in on an object, proceed as follows

1) Click on the Zoom tool in the toolbox.
2) Click on the magnifying glass with the plus sign in the flyout menu.
3) Place the mouse pointer, which now has the shape of a magnifying glass, at a free position nearby the object to be enlarged.
4) Drag the mouse pointer across the object until the dotted frame encloses the object to be enlarged.
5) Release the mouse button.

In fact, the object itself is not enlarged. Only the display has altered. CorelDRAW! has changed the Ruler and grid point settings according to the zoom in factor.

Zooming out, or reducing an object on screen to its orig-

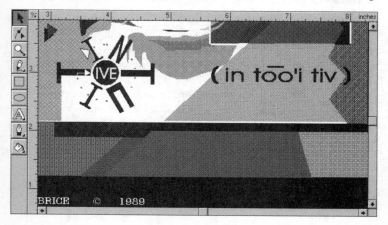

inal size, is just as simple. Open the flyout menu and select the magnifying glass with the minus sign. The display level which was last activated is again shown on the
screen.

There are scroll bars at the right-hand side and at the
bottom of the screen. You can use these (by clicking on
them) to view parts of the object which are not displayed
on the screen. Clicking on the bar itself moves the object display up or down by one screen page, clicking on
the arrow moves the object display by one line.

1.6   Outlining and filling objects

Up until now, all the objects we have dealt with have had
the same outline and filling. If you wish to change these
settings, use the Outline tool or the Fill tool.

 — Outline tool,
     — Fill tool

These tools enable you to define the line thickness,
shape and pattern or colour for the outlining, or apply filling to objects.

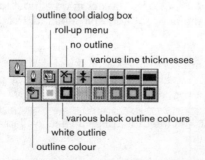

outline tool dialog box
  roll-up menu
    no outline
      various line thicknesses

various black outline colours
white outline
outline colour

Draw a simple rectangle at a free space on the screen.
You can alter the outline of the object as follows:

1)   Select the rectangle.
2)   Click on the Outline tool in the toolbox.
3)   In the flyout menu, select the thickest line by click-
     ing on the button at the extreme right of the menu.

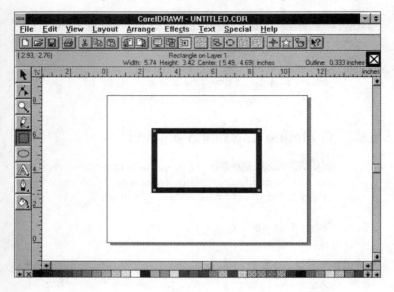

You can apply filling to the object in an almost identical
way. The rectangle is probably still selected. Proceed as
follows:

1)   Click on the Fill tool.
2)   Select a grey tint from the flyout menu by clicking
     on the appropriate button in the lower row.

We shall deal with the other possibilities available in the
flyout menu later.

1.7   Working with menus

We have mentioned the menubar previously. There are nine menus on the menubar:

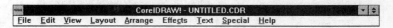

Each menu provides a number of functions and commands. We shall discuss how they work, using the *Layout* menu as an example. To open a menu, click on the name of the menu on the menubar. The menu opens, providing a list of options:

If you wish to select a certain option, simply click on it. Imagine that you wish to alter the page layout which determines the way the document comes out of the printer. Proceed as follows:

1) Click on *Layout* in the menubar. The menu opens.
2) Click on the *Page Setup* option in the menu. The dialog window on the next page appears:
3) Make changes by, for example, changing the orientation from Portrait (the image is placed vertically on the paper) to Landscape (the image is placed horizontally on the paper).
4) Then click on the *OK* button. The page layout on the screen is changed according to the new settings.

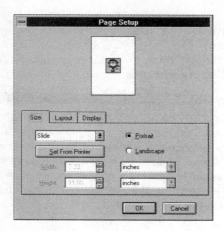

This type of dialog window also appears in the other menus. If you specify a different setting and you wish to revoke your decision, you can always click on the *Cancel* button. In the Appendices, there is an outline of how to work with dialog windows, along with a summary of commands that can be invoked by means of buttons and shortcut keys.

1.8 Closing down CorelDRAW!

Finally in this chapter, we shall describe two essential tasks: saving your work and closing down the program in the proper way.

1.8.1 Saving a drawing

There are two methods of saving an image in Corel-DRAW!. You can either open the *File* menu and select the *Save* option, or you can choose to close down the program. If you close down the program without saving (the last modifications to) your drawing, CorelDRAW!

will automatically ask if you want to save the changes, so that you will not unintentionally lose any of your work.

However, it is very advisable to save your drawing at regular intervals while you are working. This will prevent losing any work if there is a power cut or other electrical disturbance, or if the computer 'jams' for any reason. The computer may jam if you are working with several programs simultaneously under Windows and the computer working memory cannot cope with all the demands. In that case, all unsaved information will be lost irretrievably, since it is only stored in working memory and not on disk(ette).

In addition, keep in mind that when you save an image under a previously used name, the previous version is saved as a backup with the extension BAK. For instance, imagine you draw a circle and save it under the name CIRCLE.CDR. Then you add an ellipse to the drawing and save it again under the same name. The first version, containing only the circle, is saved as a backup version with the name CIRCLE.BAK. Then you add a text to the drawing and save it again under the same name. The CIRCLE.CDR file will contain the most recent drawing (circle, ellipse and text) and the previous version (with circle and ellipse) will be allocated the name CIRCLE.BAK. The very first version (circle only) will then be deleted.

As mentioned, CorelDRAW! provides two different methods of saving a drawing. We shall describe how you save a drawing for the first time:

1) Open the *File* menu by clicking on the menubar.
2) Select the *Save* or *Save As* command. If you have not saved the drawing previously, it will make no difference which you choose. The *Save Drawing* dialog box appears:

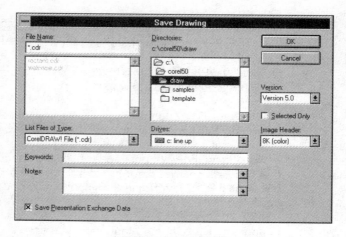

3) Specify the required directory in the *Directories* list. (If you wish to create a new directory for your drawings, switch to the Program Manager under Windows, then activate the File Manager in the Main group, open the *File* menu there and select *Create Directory*; specify the new directory name and path.)

4) Type the new name for the file in the *File Name* text box (maximum of eight characters).

5) Click on *OK*.

CorelDRAW! then saves the drawing in its present form. However, the drawing is still available in working memory and is still shown on the screen. If you now make alterations to the drawing and wish to save the drawing again, open the *File* menu and select *Save*. You need make no further specifications, CorelDRAW! already knows the file name and the directory in which the file is stored. The version on disk is replaced by the most recent version. The previous version then becomes the backup, as described above.

But you can also choose the *Save As* option again. In
that case, you can specify a different name for the file
and even select a different directory in which to store it.
In this way, you can store various versions of a drawing
under various names.

1.8.2 Closing down CorelDRAW! and saving a drawing

When you wish to close down CorelDRAW!, open the
File menu and select the *Exit* command. If the drawing
has not yet been saved or if alterations have been made
since it was saved for the last time, the following dialog
window will appear:

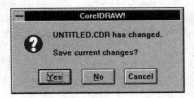

If you want to save the most recent modifications, click
on *Yes*. The *Save Drawing* dialog window appears so
that you can save the drawing under the same name or
under a new name if you wish. Click on *OK* when you
have specified how the file is to be saved.

2 CorelDRAW! Graphic tools and facilities

We shall continue the description of graphic facilities which we began in the previous chapter. Now we shall discuss in more detail the facilities for drawing and editing objects.

Firstly, we shall describe preparations for compiling a drawing CorelDRAW!. Then we shall reflect on the question of what graphic objects actually are, which properties do they have and how can they be applied in the construction of extensive and complex drawings. Subsequently, we shall deal with how various shapes such as rectangles, ellipses, lines and text can be created, edited and given a special design. At the end of this chapter, we shall give an indication as to which facilities are available for allocating various contours and filling to existing objects.

The topics in this chapter:

- specifying the page setup
- specifying the display settings
- working with guide lines and the Zoom function
- creating graphic objects
- selecting objects
- using the Pick tool to edit objects (moving, scaling, rotating and skewing)
- shaping objects using the Shape tool
- editing object outlines
- creating filling and gradient fills (colour) and allocating these to objects.

2.1 Preparation

Prior to creating a drawing in CorelDRAW!, it may be useful to make alterations to the default settings in the program in order to adjust CorelDRAW! to your particular requirements. You must first determine the page layout, the display settings, and become familiar with the Zoom function and using guide lines.

2.1.1 Determining the Page Setup

Normally, a drawing is presented on paper. But it is also possible to display a drawing on the screen as a part of a (video) presentation. Regardless of the type of display, you must also think about the orientation and the page format of the drawing. The default settings in CorelDRAW! are geared to placing drawings on paper and certain page settings are required for this. These settings determine the orientation (vertical or horizontal) and the size of the paper on which the drawing is to be printed. To adjust these, proceed as follows:

1) Click on the *Layout* menu on the menubar.
2) Choose the *Page Setup* option. The *Page Setup* dialog window appears (see overleaf).

The *Page Setup* dialog window contains three tabsheets. On the Size tabsheet, you can specify the page orientation (Portrait or Landscape, in other words, vertical or horizontal). You can also specify the paper size here, such as Letter, Legal, Tabloid etc. You can also define your own size if you wish. In that case, you can do this in the desired units of measurement such as inches, millimetres, picas or points.

If you use CorelDRAW! to create slides for a presentation and wish to export these to a video show, select the

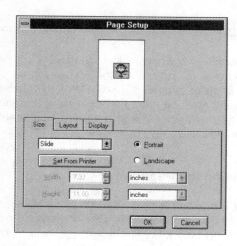

Slide option from the list. This defines a page whose height/width ratio is the same as a 35 mm slide.

We have chosen the following settings for the examples in this book:

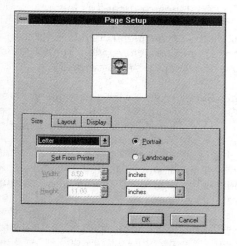

If you wish to try out the examples in this book, adopt these settings by changes the relevant settings in the *Page Setup* window.

This dialog window provides additional options. The Display tabsheet, for instance, enables you to determine the colour of the paper and the page borders. Click on this tabsheet and then on the Paper Color box. You can then specify a colour for the preview window in which you are working. This colour is not printed, it is only used to give a coloured background to the preview window. White is the default setting for this. Click on a different colour in the colour palette which opens up, such as blue for instance. An example of the specified colour is shown in a small figure at the top of the dialog window. This option is convenient if you are going to print your drawing on coloured paper; you can then get an idea of what the result will be. Switch back to white so that the following alterations will be clear.

If you want to specify a coloured background which will actually be printed, click on the Add Page Frame button. No changes are shown on the screen initially, but when you click on *OK* and the dialog window is closed, the page frame settings take effect (see the figure overleaf).

A frame has been allocated to the page, exactly the same size as the page. This is indicated by the four small blocks shown.

However, if this were now to be printed, the page would still be white. If you want to allocate a colour or a grey tint to this frame so that this will also be printed, you have to actively specify this. If the page is no longer active (with the four blocks), click on the Pick tool and then on the frame to activate it. Select a colour from the colour palette or a filling from the Fill tool flyout menu. The page will then be printed with the colour or pattern or shading.

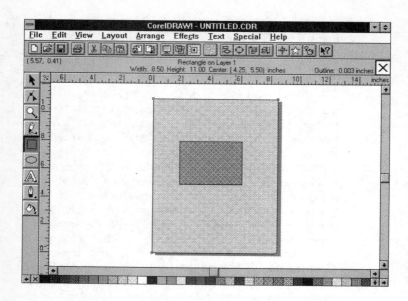

Thus, in other words, the Add Page Frame button enables you to create a printable frame or background for
the drawing but you have to specify the colour or shading after you have activated this option. Keep in mind
that the page frame option on its own only produces the
black border you saw in the print preview window on the
screen.

There is yet another way of displaying a page border.
This option is also shown on the Display tabsheet in the
Page Setup dialog window - *Show Page Border*.

If a cross is placed in the *Show Page Border* check box,
the page size in the work area is shown as the outline.
This outline is not printed and is only meant to be used
as reference for the page size. If we place these three
options under one another, the distinctions soon become clear:

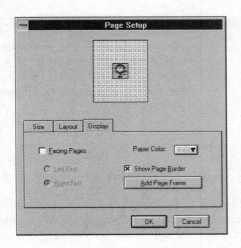

Command   Function

Paper Color

This setting is used to give the specified page a background colour which is not actually printed. Therefore, it is only useful to select a colour other than white when you want to contrast the shapes on the screen with a different colour.

Add Page Frame

This setting draws a black frame the same size as the defined page. Corel-DRAW! regards this frame as being a rectangle, which means that you can apply colours and patterns to it for example. This will be printed if you subsequently activate it and assign a colour or shading. Accordingly, you can print the entire background of the page in colour or in a grey tint. If you do not assign any colour or shading to this rectangle, no frame or background will be printed.

Show Page Border	This setting displays the defined page with a frame and a shadow border. This makes it easy to recognise the printable page in the work area. The display of the page frame does not influence the printout.

2.1.2 Display settings

You can make further standard settings for your program in the *Layout* and *View* menus. The options in these menus enable you to define a great number of settings for the screen display; you can switch these on and off as required. Open the *Layout* menu by clicking on the menubar. The following menu appears:

The last five options in the *Layout* menu refer to the screen display. These options can be activated and deactivated by simply clicking on them. You will recognise an activated option by the tick mark in front of it. Open the menu and switch all the options off and then activate them one by one so that the effects become clearly visible. We shall give a brief description of various options.

Grid and Scale Setup

When you click on this option, the following dialog window opens:

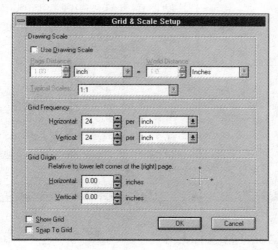

This setting determines the *Grid Origin* in relation to a chosen position in the work area. You also define the *grid frequency* here, which is the distance between the grid points. A change in the grid frequency can be useful when an object has to be positioned with great accuracy. The units of measurement for the grid are the same as the units used on the status line to indicate the positions and sizes of objects. The units of measurement used on the Rulers are also determined by those in the grid. We shall use 24 grid marks to an inch; we have specified this is the Grid Frequency section. The Grid Origin (0.0) is in the bottom left-hand corner of the page. When you activate the Show Grid option, the grid is shown in small blue points (on a colour monitor). The number of marks shown depends on the section of screen which you have chosen using the Zoom in or out functions.

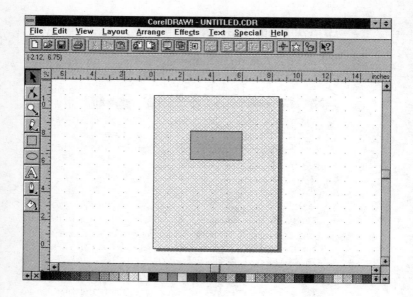

Guidelines Setup

Guidelines are useful in constructing and positioning objects accurately. When activated (see opposite), their 'magnetic' function facilitates position precision. When you move the mouse pointer to the area around a guideline, it is attracted to the line as if it were being drawn by a magnet. If, for example, various objects have to be placed next to one another, you do not need to worry too much about the exact coordinates of their positions; the objects are drawn to the nearest guideline. However, you do need to think about the exact positions of the guide lines. There are two methods of applying guidelines:

1) Open the *Layout* menu and select *Guidelines Setup*. A dialog window appears in which you can make the relevant settings. The Horizontal and Ver-

tical sections determine the respective alignment. You can specify the exact position with numerical precision in the text box. You can relocate an existing guideline by typing the new position in the text box (e.g. 8.5) and then clicking on the Move button. If you want to remove a line, specify its position and click on the Delete button. Finally, you can use the roll-up menu to display the positions of all existing guidelines and then alter, move or delete them as required.

2) Click on one of the two Rulers in the work area and drag the mouse pointer to the Drawing Window. In this way, you can position a horizontal guideline using the vertical Ruler and a vertical one using the horizontal Ruler. Drag the guideline to the required position and release the mouse button. If you wish to move a line, click on the line and drag it to a different position. To remove a guideline from the Drawing Window, click on it and drag it back to the Ruler.

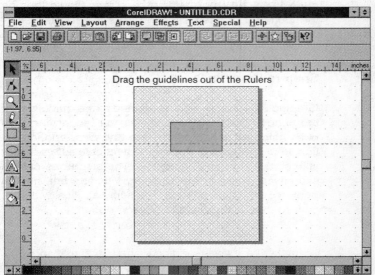

Guidelines, just like grid marks, provide the possibility of giving simple shape to graphic objects. Both features are visible on the screen but they are not printed on paper.

Snap to Grid

As mentioned, the grid is very useful when positioning or measuring objects. If you wish to align objects with great precision, it is advisable to make use of the *Snap to Grid* option in the *Layout* menu. All grid marks are then given a 'magnetic' function, which means that when you move an object for example, it is drawn to the nearest grid mark.

Due to the specified grid frequency, it may happen that a drawing action cannot be culminated between grid marks. A complicating factor may also be that not all the specified grid marks are shown on the screen; the frequency may be so great that the screen would then be too cluttered. If necessary, in cases like these, deactivate the option.

Snap to Guidelines

Graphic objects can also be aligned to the guidelines. If the *Snap to Guidelines* option from the *Layout* menu has been activated, it has priority over the *Snap to Grid* option. In the process of drawing, objects are automatically aligned to the nearest guideline. The guidelines can be placed anywhere in the Drawing Window but are not printed on the final printout. The same applies, within its own context, to the *Snap to Objects* option.

Rulers and colour palette

The Rulers and the colour palette provide even more facilities when you are constructing extensive drawings. You can activate and deactivate the Rulers as you please. Working with these makes creating an editing objects quicker and more orderly. To activate the Rulers (if they are not already shown), open the *View* menu and click on *Rulers*.

When the Rulers have been activated, another very convenient function becomes available: the *zero points*. It is very easy to make measurements when the beginning of the Ruler is exactly at the position from which the measurement has to be made. The Ruler crosshairs are used to change the zero points (Grid Origin).

1) To move the zero points of the Rulers, move the mouse pointer to the position where the Rulers join, and press and hold down the left mouse button.
2) Drag the mouse pointer to the work area. Two guidelines appear, the so-called *crosshairs*.

3)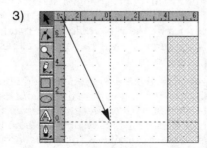

As soon as you release the mouse button, the zero points on the Rulers move automatically to align with the position of the mouse pointer. The crosshairs then disappear.

You can alter the colour palette by selecting *Color Palette* from the *View* menu. The options provided refer to the predefined colour palettes which are commonly used in the graphic world.

Wireframe View and Print Preview

The *Wireframe* and *Full-Screen Preview* options from the *View* menu refer to the Drawing Window and the Print Preview window. When you activate one of these options, the screen is redrawn. The Print Preview window is a window in which the drawing is displayed along with all the attributes for filling and outlining. It shows the drawing as it will come out of the printer. Certain PostScript facilities, such as PostScript textures, form an exception here; these can only be viewed on the paper itself. The Wireframe View only applies to the Drawing Window.

By pressing F9, the result of your work as it will come out of the printer will be shown. If you press Shift+F9, the Wireframe View is shown on the screen along with all the other program components (Rulers, menubar etc.). You can edit the outlines of objects quickly and easily in the Wireframe View. No colours or patterns are shown. If the Wireframe View is not active, all elements of the drawing are shown.

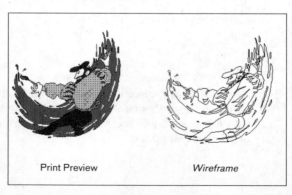

Print Preview   Wireframe

Preview Selected Only, Refresh Window

When you activate the *Preview Selected Only* in the *View* menu, only the selected objects are displayed in the Preview window. It is advisable to make use of this feature if you are working with large, complex drawings since the (re)construction of the window with each change can be very time-consuming.

If the *Refresh Window* option in the *View* menu is activated, the objects on the screen are redrawn. This option is used to remove the residue of previous actions or to continue drawing when you have switched between display modes.

Bitmaps

All imported pixel images can be displayed in the work area by activating the *Bitmaps* option in the *View* menu. Unfortunately, this does lead to a certain slowing down of the processing speed. In this mode, however, redrawing the screen in the Wireframe View is actually carried out quicker. If the function is switched off, only a bitmap frame is shown. Bitmaps are always shown in the Preview window (we shall discuss this later in more detail).

2.1.3 The Zoom function

The Zoom tool enables you to enlarge or reduce all parts of the drawing window progressively. When you click on the Zoom tool, a flyout menu appears with 6 options. Their functions are described below and their corresponding shortcut key combinations are also given:

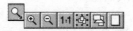

Zoom In/F2

To enlarge an object:

1) Click on the magnifying glass with the plus sign.
2) Move the mouse pointer to a position close to the object to be magnified. Press the left mouse button and drag a frame across the (part of the) object.
3) Release the mouse button.

The Drawing Window is redrawn. The magnified object now occupies the entire screen. CorelDRAW! ensures that the zoom ratio is applied in such a way that the area to be displayed, regardless of how large you made the zoom frame, fills the entire screen. A maximum enlargement factor of 12 is possible, depending on the graphic card and monitor being used.

Zoom Out/F3

Reduction in size takes place in a similar way as enlargement. By clicking on the magnifying glass with the minus sign, the screen display is changed back to how it was prior to the previous enlargement or by a factor of two if there was no previous enlargement.

Zoom Actual Size

If you click on the 1:1 button, the display is altered in such a way that one inch on the screen corresponds to an inch on paper.

Zoom To Selected/Shift+F2

This option enlarges the selected objects.

Zoom To All Objects/F4

You choose this option to show all the objects in the drawing.

Zoom To Page/Shift+F4

This option shows the page as defined in the *Page Setup* dialog window.

2.1.4 Preferences

You can specify global options for working with Corel-DRAW! by opening the *Special* menu and selecting *Preferences*. The settings you make here can be changed again later if necessary.

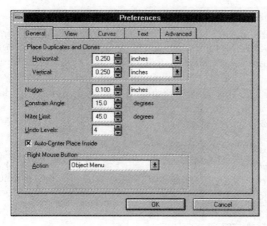

General

The *Preferences* window is subdivided into tabsheets with various interdependent options, just like other dialog windows. You can determine the following settings in the General tabsheet:

Place Duplicates and Clones This option is used to de-termine where copies of an object should be placed in relation to the original. (See also *Duplicate* in the *Edit* menu.) Positive values move the copy to the right and up-wards, negative values move it to the left and down-wards. If you enter 0.00 in both text boxes in this section, the copy is placed on top of the original.

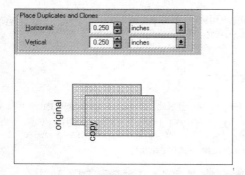

In addition, you can determine the units of measurement here in the familiar way. Click on the drop-down list if you want to define other units.

Nudge The value entered here determines the distance by which an object is moved when the cursor keys are used for this purpose. You can change the units of meas-urement here too if necessary.

Constrain Angle Controls the angle of motion when you perform any of the following actions with the Ctrl key held down:

• skewing or rotating
• drawing straight lines in Freehand mode
• adjusting control points when using the Bézier mode.

Miter Limit This option determines the appearance or corner joints. Any corner with an angle less than the specified setting will be rounded. If the corner has an angle larger than the specified setting, it will be given a sharp point. This option is aimed at avoiding thin sharp points, where the outside lines extend beyond the position of the actual corner.

Undo Levels This option defines the number of actions which can be undone by means of the *Undo* command in the *Edit* menu (Ctrl+Z shortcut key combination). You should keep in mind that the greater the number of actions that the computer has to record, the more working memory will be used.

Right Mouse Button The following drop-down list appears when you click on the arrow next to Action:

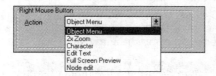

Click on one of these options to activate the relevant function for the right mouse button. The separate functions correspond to certain menu commands.

Right mouse button function	Effect in the drawing window
Object Menu	Opens a menu with options enabling you to directly implement certain settings for a selected object.
2x Zoom	Enlarges by a factor of 2. By double clicking, the drawing window is restored to the previous level.
Character	Opens the *Character Attributes* dia-

log window in which you can specify all attributes for text.

Edit Text	The *Edit Text* dialog window appears if you press the right mouse button when a text object has been selected.
Full Screen Preview	Displays a selected object in the Full Screen Preview window.
Node Edit	Activates the Shape tool to edit the selected object.

View

You can activate the following options on the View tabsheet by clicking on the appropriate check box. A cross indicates that the option has been activated. Click on the tab along the top to open the View tabsheet.

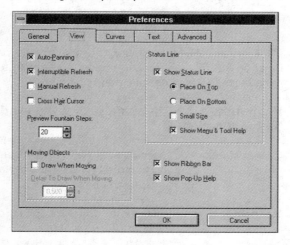

Auto-Panning When you are drawing or enlarging an object, the screen scrolls automatically to accommodate the object (size) when the object crosses the limits of the current screen window (Auto-Panning active).

You can also move objects using both the mouse and the cursor keys. But in this case, the screen does **not scroll along with the object.**

Interruptible Refresh If you often work with complex drawings, you will recognise the value of this option. When this option has been activated, you can discontinue the process of refreshing the screen at any given moment in order to isolate a certain object or to choose a tool or menu command. Then you do not need to wait until the entire drawing is displayed on the screen. The interruption is effected by pressing a random key or by clicking on the mouse. When you want to see the drawing on the screen again, open the *View* menu and select *Refresh Window.*

Manual Refresh This option allows you to manually edit screen alterations. When this option has been activated, moving an object for example, is not immediately displayed on the screen. You can then press the Ctrl+W key combination to redraw the window. It is advisable to activate this option only when you are working with extensive drawings and you do not need to continuously refresh the screen. This will save you time.

Cross Hair Cursor This option determines whether the mouse pointer is displayed as a small cross or a cross that covers the entire screen.

Preview Fountain Steps: This is where you specify the number of steps used to display the mutation of colours on the screen. If you specify a small value here (less than 15), redrawing the screen will take place more quickly but the individual steps will be clearly visible.

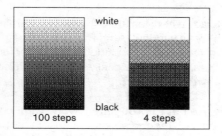

You can also activate or deactivate the status line and the Ribbon, or move these to a different position on the screen. In addition, you can determine whether or not objects should be outlined during the moving process.

Curves

When you click on the Curves tab, the following dialog window appears:

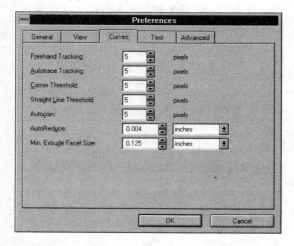

Freehand Tracking: This option enables you to specify the precision (1 to 10 pixels) with which CorelDRAW! calculates the curves for drawings created in the freehand mode. A small value means that the curve will follow each small deviation in the run of the line, making it appear more angular than when a larger value is specified.

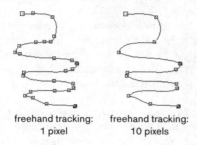

freehand tracking: freehand tracking:
1 pixel   10 pixels

Autotrace Tracking This option enables you to determine the precision with which the Bézier curve follows the edges of a bitmap (an image composed of a series of pixels or dots) traced using the autotracing feature. (Bézier curves are dealt with in section 2.3.3.) As with the Freehand Tracking, low numbers produce more accurate results.

Corner Threshold This option defines the value at which CorelDRAW! will draw a sharp or a round corner. This value applies to images drawn in the Freehand mode and in the Autotracing function.
Smaller values (1 to 3 pixels) produce sharp corners; larger values (7 to 10 pixels) produce more rounded corners.

Straight Line Threshold This option defines the threshold value at which CorelDRAW! will draw a fragment as a straight line or as a curve. This value applies to the Freehand mode and to Autotracing a bitmap. The lower the number, the greater the tendency towards drawing curves.

AutoJoin This option determines the distance between the starting and end points within which automatic joining is carried out. The lower the number, the closer the cursor must be to the end node of an existing segment in order for the next segment to automatically attach to it.

AutoReduce This option determines the extent to which the shape of the curve is changed when you use the AutoReduce option in the Node Edit roll-up menu. The higher the setting, the more nodes it moves and the more the curve's shape is changed.

Minimum Extrude Facet Size This option determines the facet size, which represents the distance between shades of colour in extrusions. A good rule of thumb is: select a high value for the facet size while working so that the screen is quickly built up; specify a low value when you come to printing to increase the quality of the printout. When you first begin to work with Corel-DRAW!, you should accept the default setting of 5 pixels until you are more familiar with the functions.

Text

Click on the Text tab to open the following dialog window:

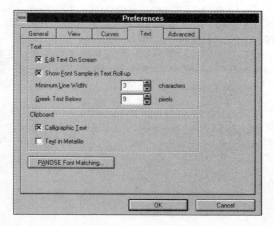

Edit Text on Screen This option determines whether you implement text editing directly in the drawing window or only in the Text dialog window.

Show Font Sample in Text Roll-Up This option determines whether a sample of the selected font is shown in the Text roll-up menu first, prior to application.

The options in the Clipboard section determine how text is copied to the Clipboard or exported. It can be copied as Calligraphic text with all pen outlines and formatting features, and made available to other programs in this way. You can also copy the text as Metatext to the Clipboard; when this option is activated, text is pasted from the Clipboard as text, meaning that font, point size and other attributes are also copied along with the text string. When deactivated, the text is pasted as curve objects.

Advanced
When you click on the Advanced tab, the following dialog window appears:

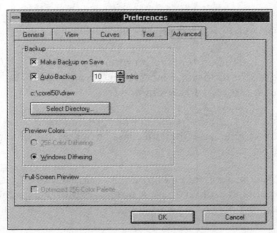

Backup The Backup section determines whether or not a backup copy with the extension .BAK should be made when the file is saved. You can also specify the interval between the automatic backups being carried out. The Select Directory button enables you to specify a directory for the backup copies.

Preview Colors and *Full-Screen Preview* These sections determine the colour display on the screen. You can only use these settings if your graphic card and monitor are capable of displaying 256 colours at one time. In addition, you require the corresponding Windows driver for this.

2.2   Graphic objects

When we discuss graphic objects, we refer in general to lines, rectangles, ellipses and texts. But what are graphic objects exactly and which features characterise them? In order to give an answer, we have to introduce two new terms: *pixel-based drawing* and *object-based drawing*. The latter is also referred to as *vector graphics*.

Pixel-based graphics

A pixel-based graphic program is one like the Windows graphic program, Paintbrush. CorelPHOTO-PAINT is also a pixel-based program.

When you draw a line in Paintbrush and zoom in closely on it, you see that this line is made up of individual points.

This not only applies to lines, it applies to all basic elements in a drawing. In a pixel-based drawing, each separate point can be edited. The smaller the points, the

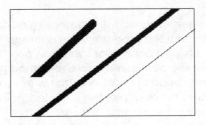

greater the resolution and the sharper the drawing. The display of the points on the screen corresponds to the points on the printout later.

A disadvantage of pixel-based graphic elements is that hidden elements are lost. Examine the following image:

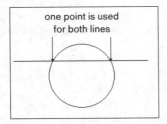

The position at which the lines intersect is defined by one independent point. There is no possibility of distinguishing between an upper or lower line. All points are situated on the same two-dimensional surface. The point which is drawn most recently deletes any other point it comes to overlap.

Imagine that the first line is blue. A second, red line is drawn in such a way that it overlaps the first line at various positions. A pixel-based program does not recognise lines, only collections of points. As mentioned, if one point comes to overlap another, the first point is deleted. Thus, the red line will delete any blue points it overlaps. There will be no purple points. The disadvantages of this will be clear.

Because the components of the drawing are made up of separate points and the program does not regard them as forming a coherent entity, a drawing can only be edited by means of the points, not by means of the graphic objects they represent. This means that with reduction and enlargement for example, the selected points can only be modified in fixed steps.

Another disadvantage is that the memory and disk capacity required increases with the size of the drawing and the number of colours applied.

Pixel-based graphic programs do provide clear advantages when the user is busy creating impressionist or expressionist works of art.

The above-mentioned problems do not arise with object-based graphics.

Object-based graphics

In contrast to pixel-based graphics, lines, curves, rectangles, ellipses etc. in an object-based graphic program are recognised as such and are defined by *vectors*. Object-based programs are often referred to as *vector* graphic programs. The drawings are actually stored as combinations of mathematical equations. Any object can be edited in terms of size, colour or shape at any given moment without other objects being modified or removed. Objects can be placed 'under' or 'above' other objects. One could refer to a three-dimensional drawing area (see the figure on the following page).

The most important advantage of the vector structure lies in the possibility of altering the measurements of an object as you please. An object-based drawing can be enlarged or reduced without any loss of quality. Other

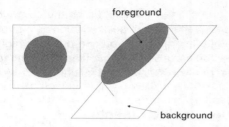

modifications, such as altering the outline or the pattern, can be easily applied.

In addition, these drawings generally occupy less disk and memory space than pixel-based graphics, although this does not apply to very complex vector graphics. Extensive colour palettes, on the other hand, do not require much additional disk and memory capacity.

CorelDRAW!, which is basically a vector-based program, attempts to make an optimal combination of these two concepts. The CorelTRACE program is supplied with the CorelDRAW! package and this program enables you to convert pixel images to vector images. We shall give a small example to illustrate this:

When you begin working with drawings more intensively, you will probably first make sketches on paper prior to creating the images on the screen.

You can then scan these sketches. The result will almost always be a pixel image. You can apply the CorelTRACE program to convert these pixel images to vector-based objects. The computer can then be used to edit the objects as you please.

The computer is much quicker in making changes than you would be when working manually. For instance, colouring a drawing on paper is much more time-consuming than giving a few commands on the computer. And using professional output devices such as a photosetter and a colour laser printer, you can produce high-quality drawings. You can also take your files to a printing firm to have them printed on advanced machinery.

2.3 Creating graphic objects

CorelDRAW! has four basic tools for constructing complex images: the Freehand tool, the Rectangle, the Ellipse and the Artistic Text tool. These tools are shown as icons in the toolbox on the left-hand side of the screen, and can be activated by clicking on these icons. The tools have their own default settings, such as colour, line thickness etc. but these can be changed to suit your own requirements.

Switch off the Wireframe View if necessary by pressing Shift+F9. Colours and grey tints will now be shown during the construction process.

2.3.1 Drawing rectangles and ellipses

We described how to draw a rectangle in chapter one. Here is a summary of the procedure:

1) Click on the Rectangle icon in the toolbox.
2) Place the mouse pointer in the drawing window at the position where the rectangle is to begin.
3) Press and hold down the left mouse button, and drag the mouse diagonally downwards to create a frame on the screen.
4) Release the mouse button when the rectangle has reached the appropriate size.

If you wish to create a perfect square, proceed as de-

scribed above, but hold down the Ctrl key while dragging the frame open. When the square has reached the
required size, first release the Ctrl key and then the
mouse button.

Ellipses and circles are drawn in a similar way:

1) Click on the Ellipse tool in the toolbox.
2) Place the mouse pointer at the position in the drawing window where the ellipse is to begin.
3) Press and hold down the mouse button and drag
   the mouse pointer in the required direction. An ellipse appears. If you wish to draw a circle, press
   and hold down the Ctrl key while dragging.
4) Release the Ctrl key first if you have used it, and
   then the mouse button.

You can also create rounded rectangles, squares and
arches. Consult section 2.5.1.

2.3.2 Drawing straight lines

You can use the Freehand tool to draw curves, freehand
lines and straight lines. Prior to clicking on the Freehand
tool in the toolbox, have a look at the icon to see which
mode is active: the Bézier mode or the freehand mode.
To change the mode hold down the mouse button a little
longer than usual when you click on the tool. A flyout
menu appears:

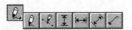

The first icon represents the Freehand mode, the second the Bézier mode. Select one of these by clicking on
it. Both are suited to drawing irregular forms with
straight lines and corners. If you wish to draw only

curves, the choice of mode depends on the precision you wish to achieve.

In the Freehand mode, you draw by clicking on the Freehand icon and dragging the mouse pointer across the drawing window. Since exact curves are almost impossible to create using the mouse, corners and sharp angles will almost inevitably appear. However, you can use the Shape tool later to round these off.

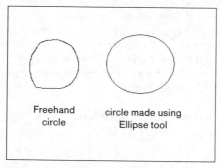

Freehand
circle

circle made using
Ellipse tool

In the Bézier mode, a drawing is created by linking the individual points. You determine the starting and end points of the curve which CorelDRAW! subsequently joins. Because you can guide the small blocks while drawing, it is possible to draw even curves. Therefore, if you wish to work accurately, it is advisable to use this mode.

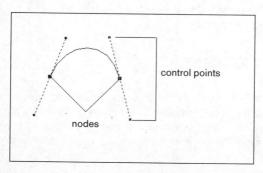

control points

nodes

In the Freehand mode, a straight line is drawn as follows:

1) Click on the Freehand tool icon. Select the Freehand mode if necessary.
2) Place the mouse pointer at the position in the drawing window where the straight line is to begin. Click once.
3) Move the mouse pointer to the required end point and click again.
4) If the straight line is to be extended, click on the end point again and then specify another end point by clicking as you did above. Separate straight lines can be extended in this way.

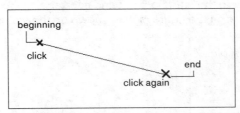

If you do not exactly touch on the end point of the straight line, this need not be a problem. CorelDRAW! accepts a deviation of 5 pixels (see the AutoJoin option in the *Preferences* dialog window, opened via the *Special* menu). You can alter this value if necessary.

If you hold down the Ctrl key while drawing a straight line, the line will be placed horizontally or vertically at an angle of 15° relative to the original point, or a multiple of this.

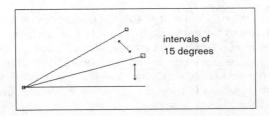

To draw a straight line in the Bézier mode, proceed as follows:

1) Click on the Freehand tool icon and select the Bézier mode if necessary.
2) Place the mouse pointer at the position where the straight line is to begin and click once.
3) Move the mouse pointer to the position where the straight line is to end and click again.
4) If the straight line is to be extended, move the mouse pointer to the next end point and click again.

If you wish to create a closed form, move the mouse pointer to the starting point and click again. The number of nodes in the figure is then shown on the status line.

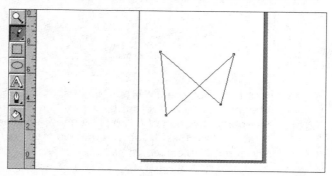

2.3.3 Drawing curves and freehand lines

Curves and freehand lines are comparable. A curve of a circle will be immediately regarded as a curve, while a signature will be seen as a freehand line. However, the signature consists of various curves. We shall again make a distinction between the Freehand mode and the Bézier mode. Curves are drawn as follows in the Freehand mode:

1) Click on the Freehand tool icon and select the Free-hand mode if necessary.
2) Place the mouse pointer in the drawing window and click on the left mouse button. Hold the button down and draw the curve.
3) Release the mouse button at the end point of the curve.

If you wish to draw another curve which is linked to the first one, simply begin the new curve at the end point of the first one (within a distance of 5 pixels if possible); CorelDRAW! will then automatically join them.

In the Bézier mode, proceed as follows:

1) Click on the Freehand tool icon and select the Bézier mode if necessary.
2) Place the mouse pointer at the position where the curve is to begin.
3) Click on the left mouse button. A block appears, marking the starting point of the curve.
4) Click and hold down the mouse button at the position where the curve is to end. A dotted line appears. Drag the mouse pointer across the drawing window. You will see that the blue dotted line moves with the mouse pointer. The distance of the mouse pointer from the original click position determines the height or depth of the curve, the angle of the blue line on the screen determines the slope of the curve.
5) Release the mouse button when the curve has acquired the required shape.
6) You can then continue the curve by clicking on another position on the screen and holding down the mouse button. A curve is automatically drawn to this position. You can modify the curve by dragging the mouse pointer across the screen as in step 4.

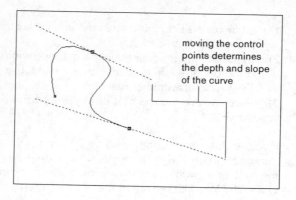

moving the control points determines the depth and slope of the curve

You can repeat the last three steps as many times as you wish. If you want to draw a closed form (so that you can fill it in for example), click on the first block once again. If you wish to draw a curve which is not connected to the previous curve, press the spacebar twice before clicking on the starting point of the new curve.

If you wish to add an extension to an existing curve or other graphic object, proceed as follows:

1) Select the object which is to be extended by clicking on it using the Pick tool.

2) Click on the Freehand tool.

3) Place the mouse pointer on the block from which the new curve extension is to be made, and click.

4) Click and hold down the mouse pointer at another point in the drawing window to mark the end point of the new curve. Drag the curve until the required shape is created.

5) Repeat step 4 if you wish to extend the object further.

2.3.4   Dimension tools

Dimension tools are frequently used in technical drawing. If you wish to measure objects when working in CorelDRAW!, you can make use of the icons which are
stored behind the Freehand tool. Click on the Freehand
tool and hold down the mouse button a little longer than
usual. The flyout menu appears.

The icons in this flyout menu enable you to draw vertical,
horizontal or angled measuring lines. Make sure to
choose the proper line for the function you require. If
you try to draw a vertical dimension line by means of the
horizontal dimension tool for example, the result will be
zero. To draw a dimension line, proceed as follows:

1) Click on the Freehand tool and hold down the
   mouse button.
2) Select one of the dimension line icons in the flyout
   menu.
3) Open the *Layout* menu and select *Snap to Objects*.
   This is not absolutely necessary but it does make
   exact measurement a bit easier.
4) Click on the position where you wish to begin measuring. Move the mouse pointer to the end point of
   the measurement. A line is drawn between these
   two points. Information about the starting point and
   current end point is shown on the status line.
5) Click on the required end point. If you have activated the *Snap to Objects* option, the mouse pointer
   will be automatically attached to the end point of the
   line.
6) Move the mouse to just above or below or to the left
   or right of this end point and click again. This determines the position of the measurement registration

in the drawing window. You can see this clearly by clicking on the Zoom In tool and clicking on the measurement registration.

2.3.5 Creating text

The Artistic Text tool enables you to add text objects to a drawing. CorelDRAW! distinguishes between three sorts of text:

- artistic text
- paragraph text
- symbols

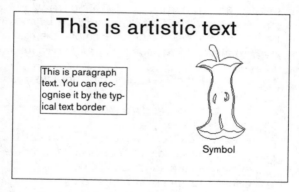

We discussed artistic text in chapter 1. We shall give a short summary of how to apply it:

Activate the Artistic text icon and click on the position in the drawing window where the text is to begin. A text cursor appears, and you can begin typing the text. (If this does not seem to work, open the *Special* menu, select *Preferences*, activate the Text tabsheet and place a cross in the Edit Text on Screen check box.) If you want to continue typing on a new line, press Enter.

CorelDRAW! provides two ways of editing text: by means of the roll-up menu which allows you to make quick changes, and by means of the options in the *Text* menu.

Roll-up menu Open the roll-up menu by pressing Ctrl+F2 or double clicking on the Text tool. This menu can be moved to a more suitable position on the screen if necessary. To do this, click on the title bar and drag the menu to another position. Then release the mouse button.

To assign attributes to a text by means of the roll-up menu, you first have to select the text using the Pick tool. Then specify the required settings in the roll-up menu and click on the Apply button.

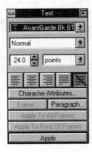

To close the roll-up menu, double click on the small button in the upper left-hand corner of the menu. If you click on the small triangle in the upper right-hand corner, the menu will roll up so that it occupies less screen space but is nevertheless readily available. Click once more to roll it down.

Character Attributes This dialog window is opened by selecting Character from the Text menu or by pressing the Ctrl+T key combination.

This dialog window contains editing options which correspond to the options behind the Attributes button in the roll-up menu. However, for the sake of brevity, we shall restrict ourselves to the creation of text and text symbols, and we shall describe the most important applications for the three sorts of text mentioned.

Creating artistic text
1) Activate the Artistic text tool by clicking on the appropriate tool icon.
2) Click on the position in the drawing window at which the text should begin.
3) Type the text.

Artistic text can be edited just as text in word processors:

Key	Function
Backspace	Deletes the character to the left of the cursor.
Del	Deletes the character to the right of the cursor, or the selected characters.
Enter	Forces a line break; the cursor is placed on the following line.
Cursor Left	Moves the cursor one character to the left.
Cursor Right	Moves the cursor one character to the right.
Home	Moves the cursor to the beginning of the current line.
End	Moves the cursor to the end of the current line.

To assign new attributes to the text, such as font, point size etc. click on the Pick tool after you have typed the text. Then select *Character* from the *Text* menu or press Ctrl+F2.

This dialog window enables you to determine the font, the point size, the character formatting and the position of the text. You can alter the size by clicking on one of the arrows to the right of the Size box, or by clicking on the box and directly entering a new size. Various fonts are provided in the Fonts list. You can move down

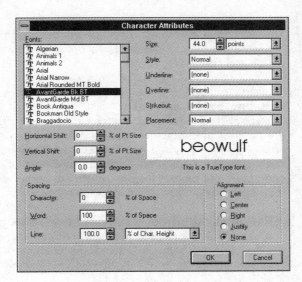

through the list by clicking on the scroll arrows. Click on a font to select it. A sample of the specifications is shown in the samples box in the dialog window.

The dialog window provides the following options:

The drop-down lists, Size, Underline, Overline, Strikeout and Placement enable you to format the text with these attributes. Select one of these by clicking on one of the options in the drop-down list.

The Fonts list displays all the fonts available in Corel-DRAW!. Select one of these by clicking on it.

You can determine the size of the selected font by clicking on the arrows to move to the required size (from 30 inches, 2160 points, down to 0.01 inches, 0.7 points).

By means of the Alignment section in the lower right-hand section of the window, you can determine the alignment of the selected text in relation to the cursor.

The options in the Spacing section enable you to determine the spacing in percentages between characters, words and lines.

Creating paragraph text

Paragraph text distinguishes itself from artistic text by the number of characters that can be displayed at one time. Artistic text has a maximum of 8,000 characters, while paragraph text can deal with multiples of 8,000 characters per block. However, there are certain editing restrictions which apply to paragraph text:

- Paragraph text can only be edited to a limited extent using the functions provided by the *Effects* menu.
- When the text frame is skewed, the characters themselves are not slanted; only the beginning of the line is shifted.

Paragraph text is entered as follows:

1) Click on the Artistic Text icon and hold down the mouse button a little longer than usual. The flyout menu appears.
2) Select the Paragraph Text icon, the right-hand icon in the menu.
3) Move the mouse pointer to the position in the drawing window where the upper left-hand corner of the paragraph frame is to appear and press the left mouse button. Drag the mouse pointer downwards to the right to specify the size of the text frame.
4) Release the mouse button. A text cursor appears.
5) Type the text.

When the text becomes
too long to fit on one
line, it is wrapped to the
next one

CorelDRAW! calculates the screen layout and displays the text within the defined frame. Thus, the text is restricted by the text border. If a word does not fit on to one line, it is automatically wrapped to the next line. If you wish to force a line break, press Enter.

You can also change the layout of paragraph text in the same way as you can change artistic text. There are many functions available for this. You can also import existing text, from Word or Word Perfect for instance, into the paragraph frame. To do so, select the paragraph text frame and open the *File* menu. Select *Import*. Specify the required file in the subsequent dialog window. The text frame will be automatically enlarged to accommodate the imported text, and if the text is very lengthy, additional pages will be added automatically.

Text symbols

In previous versions of CorelDRAW! is was possible to utilise text symbols. CorelDRAW! 5.0 still provides a library of symbols though this is no longer to be found in the toolbox. It has been added to the *Special* menu. Because these symbols are part of letter families, like Wingdings for instance, we shall give a brief description of text symbols here in this section concerning text.

Proceed as follows to insert one of these text symbols into your work:

1) Open the *Special* menu and select *Symbols Roll-Up*. The corresponding roll-up menu appears.
2) Select the required group of symbols by clicking on the small arrow next to the first group name under the title bar and then on the appropriate name in the list.
3) You can browse through the available symbols in the special manual supplied along with the Corel-

DRAW! package, and select a particular symbol by typing its number in the # text box. You can also select a symbol by opening the relevant group and clicking on the symbol.

4) Specify the size of the symbol in the Size box.
5) Click on the required symbol and drag it to the drawing window.

These text symbols can be edited just like any other graphic objects: enlarged, reduced, mirrored etc. This is due to the CorelDRAW! concept in which all graphic elements are regarded as being objects, so that all facilities are available for editing them.

2.4 Editing graphic objects

You must select graphic objects in order to be able to edit and alter them. The procedure is similar to that applied when you edit text using a word processor. To select objects in CorelDRAW!, you make use of the Pick tool. This tool enables you to move, rotate, stretch and shrink, enlarge and reduce objects. We discussed these functions in section 1.4.1 but we shall again give a brief summary here, along with tips about how to make the most efficient use of the Pick tool.

To activate the Pick tool, click on it in the toolbox, so that it looks like the icon has been pressed down. In the following description, we presume that the Pick tool has been activated.

2.4.1 Selecting objects

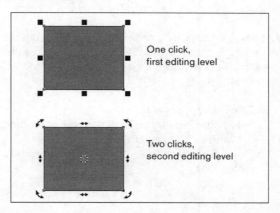

One click,
first editing level

Two clicks,
second editing level

To select an object, move the mouse pointer to any point on the outline of the object and press the left mouse button. If you click once more, the second editing level is activated, in which you can rotate and skew the object.

You can select several objects at once by means of the selection frame or by using the Shift key.

Selection frame
You can select several objects at once dragging a frame across the objects.

Shift key
If the objects are situated on the screen in such a way that it is inconvenient or impossible to select them by dragging a frame across them, you can use the Shift key to make a direct selection. This is done by holding down the Shift key and then clicking on the required objects one by one. The status line indicates how many objects have been selected. The objects themselves are surrounded by selection blocks. If you hold down the Shift key and click on a selected object, the selection is undone. If you wish to undo the entire selection, click on an empty position anywhere in the drawing window.

A drawing normally consists of a large number of objects which may be difficult to identify and select. Proceed as follows to get a good overview of the objects in your drawing:

1) Click on any object.
2) Press the Tab key several times. Each object in the drawing will be separately selected.
3) Press Shift+Tab to switch back to the previously selected object.

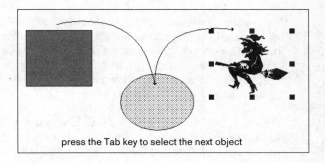

press the Tab key to select the next object

2.4.2 Moving objects

Moving objects is quite easy. Select one or more objects and click on any point on the outline of any of the objects. Hold down the mouse button. When you move the mouse, a blue frame appears. Drag this to the required position on the screen and release the mouse button. If you hold down the Ctrl key while dragging, the objects can only be moved in a horizontal or vertical direction.

If you press the plus key on the numeric keypad (one quick press is enough) while dragging the object, the original object remains where it is and a copy is made at the position where you release the mouse button. This process is referred to as *duplication*.

2.4.3 Stretching, shrinking, enlarging and reducing objects

When you first select an object, the first editing level is activated. The object is then enclosed by eight small blocks. By clicking on one of these blocks, you can stretch or shrink the object, or proportionally enlarge or reduce it.

When objects are stretched or shrunk, this means that the shape of the object is altered in a certain direction. The relative proportions change. If an object is proportionally enlarged or reduced, the height and width of the object are simultaneously altered in such a way that their mutual ratio remains the same.

While you are performing these actions, take a look at the status bar. The stretch, shrink, enlarge and reduce percentages are shown. If you stretch or alter the size of an object for a second or subsequent time, the figures refer to the changes in relation to the previous size. Alterations prior to this are forgotten.

The Ctrl key has a special significance here too. If you hold down this key while stretching or enlarging, the object is changed in steps of 100%. If you wish to make an exact mirror image of the object, move the mouse pointer to one of the blocks. The mouse pointer changes into a cross. Press and hold down the Ctrl key. Click on one of the black blocks and drag the mouse pointer across the object. A blue frame moves to the new (mirrored) position. Release the mouse button and then the Ctrl key.
If you wish to leave a copy of the object behind, proceed as described above, and when the mirroring frame has been created at the required position, click once on the right mouse button. Release the left mouse button and then the Ctrl key.

If you wish to stretch or enlarge an object from its central point, press and hold down the Shift key while dragging one of the black blocks.

If you wish to retain a copy of the original during all these manouevres, press the plus key on the numeric keypad.

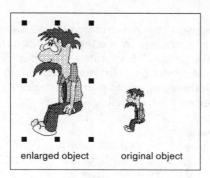

enlarged object   original object

2.4.4   Rotating and skewing objects

If you double click on an object, a frame indicating the
second editing level appears around it. This level is recognisable by the arrows. If you click on the outline of the
object, the first editing level is activated again. Each
click switches the editing level.

You can rotate and skew objects at the second editing
level. This is done by clicking on the double-headed arrows around the object.

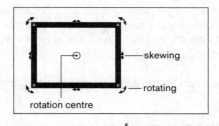

Click on a curved arrow to rotate the object or on a
straight arrow to skew the object. Drag the frame which
subsequently appears in the required direction. Release
the mouse button when the rotation or skewing has obtained the desired shape.

When rotating, you can move the rotation centre from the middle of the object to another position. This ensures that the object will be rotated around a different axis. To move the rotation point (the small circle in the middle of the object), simply click on it and drag it to the required position.

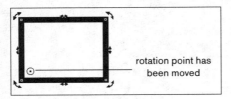

rotation point has been moved

If you press and hold down the Ctrl key while rotating and skewing, the alterations to the position of the object are made in steps of 15°. If you hold down the Ctrl key while moving the rotation axis, this point can only be placed on one of the eight handles or exactly in the middle of the object.

2.4.5 Repeating or undoing procedures

The *Repeat* command from the *Edit* menu enables you to apply the last command to another selected object. You can also press the Ctrl+R shortcut key combination for this. In chapter 3, we shall explain how to use a macro to implement various recurring actions.

If you wish to undo the previous action, press Ctrl+Z.

2.5 Reshaping graphic objects

If you wish to make alterations to the basic shape of an object, you can make use of the Shape tool. Various actions are possible, depending on the type of object. For example, you can round off rectangles, slice ellipses, and respace texts etc.

The nodes and control points of the objects form the basis for these changes. The figure below explains these terms in more detail:

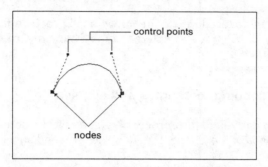

You must select an object before you can edit it by means of the Shape tool. Then click on the Shape tool. The mouse pointer assumes the form of a triangular arrow. The blocks around the selected object and the object nodes are displayed. The form and position of these nodes depend on the type of object.

If no object has been selected, or if you wish to select a different object, you only need to click on a random point of the outline of the object to activate it. When you have done this, the status line indicates the object type.

You can only edit one object at a time with the Shape tool. But if you are working with text or freehand lines, it is possible to select one or more nodes by clicking on them while holding down the Shift key or by using the marquee frame. The selected nodes are then displayed as filled black blocks.

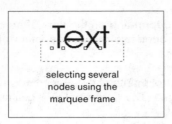

selecting several
nodes using the
marquee frame

In the following description, we shall presume that the object has been selected and the Shape tool has been activated.

2.5.1 Reshaping rectangles and ellipses

You can round the corners of rectangles and squares by means of the Shape tool. To do so, proceed as follows:

1) Use the triangular pointer to select the rectangle or square.
2) Drag one of the corner nodes along one of the sides. The further you drag the node, the rounder the corner becomes.

You can also round the corners of rectangles and squares which have been stretched and skewed.

When working with circles and ellipses, you can use the Shape tool to create arches and wedges:

1) Use the triangular pointer to select the ellipse or circle.
2) There is only one node on the outline. Drag it along the existing outline. The node divides into two so that a curve or an arch is created.
3) Dragging the nodes enables you to change the shape and length of the curve.

Depending on the position of the mouse pointer during the dragging process, a curve or a wedge will be created. If the mouse pointer is moved within the boundary of the ellipse, a wedge is created; if the mouse pointer is outside the ellipse, a curve appears.

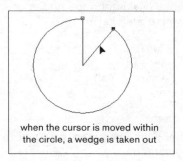

when the cursor is moved within
the circle, a wedge is taken out

If you perform these actions while holding down the Ctrl key, changes are made in steps of 15°.

2.5.2   Reshaping freehand lines

CorelDRAW! provides various possibilities for reshaping freehand lines, although the procedure itself remains the same. First use the Shape tool to select the curve or freehand line by clicking on any point on the line. The nodes are then displayed. Select the required node by clicking on it. The lines which run through this node can now be edited by various functions to give them the desired shape. The function applied depends on whether:

- you select nodes,
- you move the nodes,
- you edit the nodes, or
- change the control points.

Selecting the nodes

To edit a node, you first have to select it. Place the mouse pointer at the required position and click. You can select several nodes by dragging a marquee frame across the required nodes, or by clicking on the nodes one by one while holding down the Shift key.

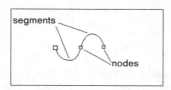

We refer to the connection between two or more selected points as a *segment*.

Moving the nodes

When you have selected the nodes or segments, you can move them by dragging them using the mouse.

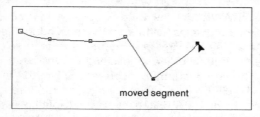

If you hold down the Ctrl key while dragging, the movement can only take place horizontally or vertically.

Changing the control points

Control points determine the amount of curve or arching between two nodes. CorelDRAW! provides the possibil-

ity of altering these. The figure below will help illustrate
the procedure:

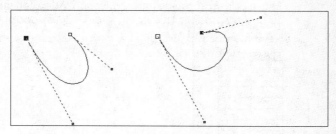

The curve at the left has two nodes, at the beginning and
at the end. Both nodes have control points, at the end of
the dotted lines. The curve at the right represents the
original curve when one of the control points has been
moved. The curve then assumes another shape.

An exact description of the relation between the control
points and the curve would demand a mathematical trea-
tise, which probably won't help you draw any better, and
is thus beyond the scope of this book. The best way to
become competent is by trying out all the possibilities.
Keep the following in mind:

- A curve always passes through the nodes.
- Each node has two control points, with the exception
  of the beginning and end nodes which only have one
  control point.
- The shape of a curve between two nodes depends on
  the position of the corresponding control point.
- The control points determine the angle at which the
  curve approaches or leaves the node.
- The greater the distance between the control point
  and the node, the deeper the curve.

Editing the nodes

The *Node Edit* roll-up menu also provides facilities for editing the nodes. This menu is opened by double clicking on one of the nodes.

The functions are activated by clicking on the buttons in the dialog window. The top row provides the following functions:

Add node (+): This option adds a new node to the selected segment.

Delete node (-): This option removes one or more activated nodes. This function can also be implemented using the Del key. Keep in mind that the control points of the adjacent nodes will determine the new shape of the segment.

Join: Select two nodes which are part of the same path. Double click on one of the nodes. The selected nodes are joined, closing an open path or making two paths into a continuous path.

Break: This option divides the curve into independent segments which each have a beginning and end point. The effect of this only becomes visible when the split nodes are moved.

Auto-Reduce: Superfluous nodes are removed without the shape of the curve being altered.

To Line: Changes the selected curve segment to a line segment.

To Curve: Changes the selected line segment to a curve segment. The control points of the new curve lie on this line, but the curve only acquires a curved shape when the control points are moved (Shape tool).

Stretch and Rotate: You can select parts of a curve and stretch and rotate it just like any other object.

Cusp: This option changes selected nodes to cusped nodes. Use this when you want to add a sharper bend to a curve, In this, the control points can be moved completely independently of one another.

Smooth: The selected nodes are changed to smooth nodes. The control points of a smooth node are always in a straight line. When a node has been changed to a smooth node, it retains this form even when one of the control points is moved. A node between two straight lines cannot be made smooth.

Align: This option aligns the selected nodes. When you activate this option, a dialog window appears in which you can specify the options Align Horizontal, Align Vertical and Align Control Points.

Symmet: The selected nodes are converted to symmetrical nodes. This produces the same curve on both sides of the node.

2.5.3 Designing sections of text

The Shape tool also enables you to edit text *typographically.* All these editing facilities can be applied to both artistic text and paragraph text.

It is not possible, however, to alter the shape of the characters with the Shape tool. If you want to do so, you will have to open the *Arrange* menu and select *Convert To Curves*. We shall give a description of the following actions:

- moving letters separately (manual kerning)
- changing the character spacing (automatic kerning)
- changing the word spacing
- changing the line and the paragraph spacing
- changing the character attributes.

B e ° w ᵤ l ꜝ	moving individual characters
B e o w u l f	altering character spacing
B e o w u l f B e o w u l f B e o w u l f	altering word spacing
Beowulf Beowulf Beowulf Beowulf Beowulf Beowulf	altering line spacing
B e ● w ⸮ **1** ꜰ	altering character attributes

Moving letters: manual kerning

You can use the Shape tool to move any letter in a text. Proceed as follows:

1) Select the text by clicking on the Shape tool. A node appears under each letter, at the left.

2) Move the triangular mouse pointer to a letter node. Click and hold down the mouse button. The status line indicates the current coordinates of the shift being carried out.

3) Drag the letter to the required position. During dragging, the letter is displayed in dotted outline so that you can see where to place it.

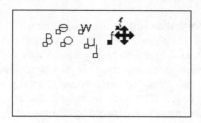

Moving separate letters on the line is referred to as manual kerning. If you hold down the Ctrl key while moving the letters, they will be kept on the same horizontal line, in other words, with no vertical deviation.

Altering the character spacing: automatic kerning

You can use a spacing symbol to change the spacing between all the characters. This is referred to as automatic kerning.

altering the character spacing

The figure shows a text which has been selected using the Shape tool. The spacing symbol, with three vertical lines, is shown to the right of the word. To adjust the spacing between all the letters, proceed as follows:

1) Use the Shape tool to select the text.
2) Click on the spacing symbol behind the selected text, and hold down the mouse button.
3) Move the mouse pointer to the left or to the right to increase or decrease the spacing between the letters. A dotted frame indicates the width of the object. When you release the mouse button, the text acquires the newly-specified spacing.

Altering the word spacing

Changing the word spacing is done in a way similar to changing the character spacing. If you hold down the Ctrl key while you drag the character spacing symbol, the space between the words is increased or decreased, depending on the dragging direction.

Altering the line and paragraph spacing

You can alter the vertical spacing in much the same way as the horizontal spacing, to adjust the spacing between lines and paragraphs. To do so, drag the vertical spacing symbol, situated to the left of the text, until the dotted line reaches the required position.

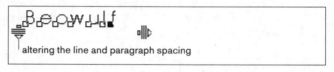

altering the line and paragraph spacing

If you hold down the Ctrl key while dragging the vertical spacing frame, the paragraph spacing within a text section is altered.

Altering character attributes

The Shape tool enables you not only to alter the spacing between characters, lines and paragraphs, you can also change the following attributes for words and groups of words:

• the font itself
• character formatting
• font size
• horizontal or vertical movement
• angle of placement.

To do so, proceed as follows:

1) Use the Shape tool to select one or more characters.
2) Double click on a selected node next to a character.
   The *Character Attributes* dialog window appears.
3) Make the required adjustments.

Fonts: The font is specified in the familiar way. Select the
required font from the list by clicking on it. An example of
the new font is shown in the sample window.

Size: Specify the required size in the Size box. Type the
size or click on the arrows to increase or decrease the
value shown.

Formatting: There are various options for formatting the
font. Click on the relevant drop-down list.

Horizontal and *Vertical Shift:* These options correspond
to the manual kerning and line spacing options. You can
specify exact values in percentages in the text boxes.

Angle: This function rotates the selected characters. These are then placed at a slant with regard to their normal position on the line. Negative values in the Angle box produce clockwise rotation and position values produce anticlockwise rotation.

Alignment: The options in this section place text in relation to the text cursor.

2.6 Editing object outlines

It is important that the attributes of an object can be easily specified and adjusted. These attributes refer to certain properties of graphic objects, such as the outline and the filling. CorelDRAW! provides special tools to deal with the outline and the filling of objects:

* the Outline tool, which is represented by the pen nib
* the Fill tool, represented by the tin of paint.

2.6.1 The shape and colour of the outline

Up until now we have worked with the default settings for the colours and patterns when creating objects. If, however, you wish to change the settings for these tools, this is easily done. You have to activate the tool first by clicking on the appropriate icon.

We shall begin by modifying the outlines. Click on the Outline tool. A flyout menu appears, displaying two rows of icons. The icons on the upper row determine the shape and the thickness of the outline, the icons on the lower row determine the colour of the object outline.

The Outline Dialog and Outline Colour functions determine the features of all objects to be created or of all selected objects. The other icons provided in this menu are used for quick selection. The upper row specifies the thickness of the lines, varying from 0.003 inches to 0.333 inches. The icons on the lower line enable you to quickly select a black or white outline or grey tints ranging from 10% to 90%.

As mentioned, there are two general methods of application. If objects are selected, they will be changed to conform to the newly-specified settings. If no objects are selected, the newly-specified settings will apply to all objects which are to be created; these then become the default settings. In this case, when you specify new settings before you begin work, a dialog window appears in which you can determine to which objects the new settings are to apply (see below). The entire procedure is as follows:

Changing the default settings

1) No object should be selected.
2) Click on the Outline tool. The flyout menu appears.
3) Click on one of the icons to make a quick choice or on the *Outline Dialog* or *Outline Color* icons if you wish to make more precise settings.
4) Click on *OK* to confirm your settings. The default settings are then altered.

Changing the features of the selected object(s)

1) Select one or more objects.
2) Click on the Outline tool. The flyout menu appears.

3) Click on one of the icons to make a quick choice or on the *Outline Dialog* or *Outline Color* if you wish to make more precise settings.

4) Click on *OK* to confirm your settings. The outline of the selected object(s) is altered to correspond to the specified settings.

If no object is selected when the Outline tool is activated, the *Outline Pen* dialog window appears enabling you to determine to which type of object the settings are to apply:

Specify the type(s) by clicking on the appropriate option(s).

Graphic: The settings only apply to new graphic objects.

Artistic Text: The settings only apply to new artistic text.

Paragraph Text: The settings apply to new paragraph text objects.

2.6.2 Specifying the line thickness

If you wish to specify an exact line thickness, open the *Outline Pen* dialog window by clicking on the pen nib icon in the Outline flyout menu.

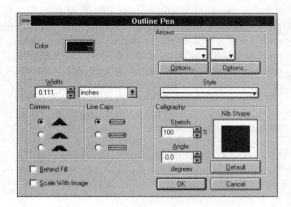

Width: Determines the width of the outline of the object. The possible values lie between 0.001 inches and 4.0 inches.

Stretch: Determines the pen shape from square to rectangular and from circular to elliptical. Possible values lie between 1% and 1000%.

Angle: Determines the angle of the pen. Possible values lie between -180° and 360°.

Default: If you click on the Default button, the values of the Stretch and Angle options are restored to the default settings, 100% and 0.0 degrees.

Nib Shape: This sample window displays the form of the pen you have specified by means of the Width, Stretch and Angle options. You can create calligraphic effects on the outline by changing the shape and angle of the nib.

Behind Fill: This option places the outline in the background and the filling in the foreground.

Scale With Image: This option ensures that the outline width and shape are automatically adjusted when the objects are enlarged or reduced. In other words, the outline is made thicker when the object is stretched and thinner when the object is shrunk.

Corners: The corner shape is determined by clicking on the appropriate option.

Line Caps: Controls how the line endings are drawn. The same selection is applied to both ends of the line/curve:

⊏⊐	Squares the line at each end;
⊂⊃	Draws round caps extending beyond the line endings;
⊏⊐	Draws square caps extending beyond the line endings

Arrows: Displays a selection of arrows you can apply to the line endings. Sixteen options are shown but you can view more by clicking on the scroll arrows. Click on the required style.

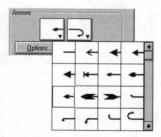

The left arrow button determines the left extremity of the arrow, the right button determines the right end. More than a hundred different arrow forms are available in the drop-down lists.

The two option buttons enable you to remove, exchange, edit the chosen arrows, or to delete them from the list.

2.6.3 Applying colours and grey tints to the outline

The outline of the object can be given a colour, can be black or white or can be a shade of grey. To specify this, click on the Outline tool and then on the *Outline Color* icon (2nd row, extreme left) of the flyout menu. You can then enter the exact settings in the subsequent dialog window. Click on the other icons instead if you wish to make quick specifications.

Just as with the outline shapes you can also change selected objects or create new default settings for objects to be created. See section 2.6.1.

If you wish to exactly specify the outline colour, click on that icon. The *Outline Color* dialog window appears:

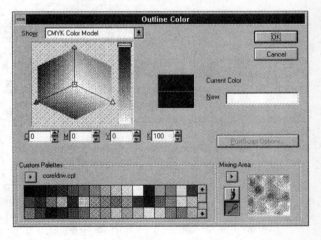

The options in this dialog window provide the following facilities:

Show: This drop-down list provides a display of the possible colours in each applicable method. Various models are available for process colouring. We shall give a brief description of the most important models (CMYK, RGB, HSB):

CMYK colour model
This model is based on the four-colour print (cyan, magenta, yellow and black).

RGB colour model
This model works on the basis of red, green and blue. A hundred percent of all colours produces black, zero percent produces white and equal percentages produce grey.

HSB colour model
This model creates colours by varying three parameters: hue, saturation and brightness.

Show Color Names: If you select commercial color models such as Pantone, Trumatch and Focoltone, or Uniform Colors, and activate the *Show Color Names* check box, a list of colour names is shown instead of a colour palette.

Mixing Area: You mix the colours from the currently active colour palette in this box. Select a color by clicking on the corresponding box and then click on the paintbrush button in the Mixing Area section. You can then transfer the colour to the mixing area by clicking on the mouse button. When you have mixed the colours to your satisfaction, click on the button under the paintbrush, the so-called Eyedropper. Move this symbol to the required colour tint in the Mixing Area and click on the mouse button. The colour under the Eyedropper is displayed in the New colour box in the middle of the dialog window. Clicking on *OK* will transfer it to the drawing window for use.

In the *Custom Palette* section, you can load different palettes, add or remove colours, save any alterations and also specify other (newly-created) palettes as the default settings if suitable.

PostScript Options: The dialog window of the same name is opened by clicking on this button. Here you can specify various halftone screens. However, these options are only useful if you have a PostScript printer.

2.7 Filling graphic objects

You can not only alter the outline of an object, you can also modify the inner surface. This Fill tool is used for this function. The settings you make when working with this tool apply to all selected objects or to objects you are about to create. The facilities for filling objects largely correspond to those used for outlining objects, as described in the previous section. Accordingly, we shall accentuate the differences here and give a brief indication of direct similarities where necessary.

When you click on the Fill tool, the flyout menu appears.

The icons on the upper row will open various dialog windows. The lower row contains options for making quick settings. You can define various shades of grey, in gradations from 10% to 90%.

2.7.1 Selecting colours and grey tints

If you wish to assign a certain grey tint to an object, or display it in black or white, click on one of the icons on the bottom row of the flyout menu. Keep in mind that the object must be selected first. If you wish to assign a colour filling, proceed as follows:

1) Click on the Fill tool in the toolbox.
2) Click on the Fill Color icon (upper row, extreme left). Choose the required colour from the subsequent dialog window.

The settings in this window are similar to those in the *Outline Color* window which we discussed above (see section 2.6.3).

2.7.2 Fountain Fill colours

Click on the Fountain Fill icon in the flyout menu. The *Fountain Fill* dialog window appears, in which you can choose the type of fountain fill and the starting and end colours for your object.

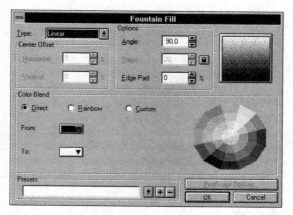

Type

Linear: Click on this option to create linear fountain fills. A linear fountain fill changes the colour in a linear way according to the specified angle of change. The result is immediately visible in the preview area.

Radial: A radial fountain fill changes the colours according to concentric circles beginning at the centre of the object. The result is immediately visible in the preview area.

Conical: A conical fountain fill resembles a round tent viewed from above, with light and shadow. The colour changes from the starting colour to the end colour in an anticlockwise direction.

Square: With a square fountain fill, the colour changes in a square pattern from the centre towards the outer parts.

Center Offset

Horizontal/Vertical: These options enable you to move the centre of a concentric fountain fill (therefore Conical, Radial and Square), so that the centre of the fountain fill is no longer the centre of the object. Negative values move the centre downwards to the left, positive values move it upwards to the right. The centre can also be moved by clicking on the desired position in the preview box.

Options

Angle: This option determines the angle of gradation in a linear, conical or square fountain fill. Select the required angle between -180° and 360°. If you click and hold down the mouse pointer in the preview area, a line appears indicating the angle of fill with regard to the centre. Move the mouse pointer to change the angle.

Steps: Click on the padlock next to this option to determine how many steps should be used to display and print the fountain fill.

Edge Pad: This option determines how large the border filling should be. It increases the amount of starting and end colour. You can also move the centre of the fountain fill by clicking on the preview area. The maximum value is 45%.

Color Blend

Direct, Rainbow, Custom: These options determine whether the fountain fill should be directly applied, in other words, from one colour spectrum to the other, or whether it should also contain all the in-between colours, as in a rainbow. The Custom option enables you to determine the intervening colours yourself.

From/To: You can determine the starting and end colours by clicking on the desired colours in the drop-down palettes. Clicking on the More button in these drop-down palettes to open a second *Fountain Fill* dialog window from which you can select the desired colour.

PostScript Options: This option opens a dialog window in which you can select one of the special PostScript halftone screens. This option is only useful if you are going to print Spot colours to a PostScript printer.

2.7.3 Two-color Fill and Full-color Fill

In addition to colours and grey tints, CorelDRAW! also provides two-colour filling and full-colour filling. You can also design your own patterns. Proceed as follows:

Two-color Fill

1) Click on the Fill tool in the toolbox. The flyout menu appears.
2) Click on the icon resembling a chess board. The *Two-Color Pattern* dialog window appears.
3) Click on the pattern to display a number of pattern options readily available. Use the scroll bar to move through the list.

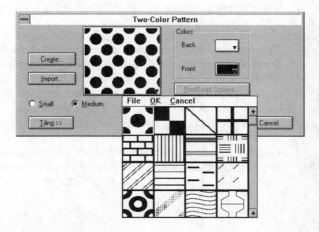

You can select a pattern by double clicking on it, or by clicking on it once and then on *OK*.

This dialog window contains a number of options for the selected pattern:

Tiling > Tile Size/Small, Medium, Large: These options determine whether or not the tiles are adjusted to preset measurements. Small means that they will be 1/4 inch square, Medium defines them as 1/2 inch square and Large makes them 1 inch square.

Tile Size/Width and Height: A pattern always consists of a large number of different patches which have been placed on an object, just like tiles in the kitchen. You can change the width and height of these by typing the required values or by clicking on the small arrows.

First Tile Offset: This option enables you to determine the starting point of the pattern in relation to the edge of the object.

Row/Column Offset: This option enables you to specify the relative positions of the tiles within the selected pattern.

Preview Box: As mentioned, you can open the list of options by clicking on the pattern shown. A drop-down list of 16 patterns appears, and you can view more by clicking on the scroll bar to the right of this list. Select the required pattern by clicking on it and then on *OK*, or by double clicking on it.

Create: You can activate the so-called Pattern Editor by clicking on this button. This enables you to create your own pattern and add it to the pattern database.

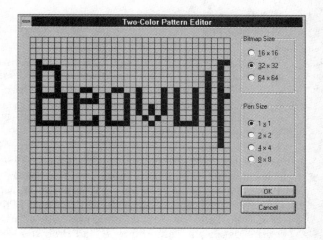

In this dialog window, you can determine the size of the
bitmap, in other words, the number of pixels, and the
size of the pen to be used to create the pattern. By clicking on the left mouse button, you place black squares in
the drawing area; by clicking on the right mouse button,
you can remove them again. Click on *OK* when you are
satisfied with the result. When you return to the *Two-Col-
or Pattern* dialog window, you can specify the foreground and background colours.

Colors/Back and Front: When you click on these buttons, a drop-down colour palette appears from which
you can choose the desired colour. You can use the
scroll bars to move through the palette. Click on Esc if
you want to leave this palette without making a choice.

Import: Click on this button to open the *Import* dialog
window. Select a file (e.g. from corel50\draw\samples
or other Windows .BMP files)) to import a pattern. You
can then modify it in the *Two-Color Pattern* window.

Full-color Fill

When you click on the Full-color Fill icon in the flyout menu, the *Full-color Pattern* dialog window appears. If you click on the pattern shown, a drop-down list of patterns opens. Click on one of these and then on *OK* to select it; you can also simply double click on it. If you click on the Load button, a list of names appears from which you can select a ready-made pattern. If you click on the Tiling>> button, you can edit the pattern displayed by means of the sizing and positioning options in the window.

You can also create patterns yourself in the drawing window by means of the normal drawing tools from the toolbox. Then open the *Special* menu and select *Create Pattern*. Specify the required type and drag the selection cross pointer across the area you wish to record as a pattern. Allocate it a suitable name. You can always retrieve it again for use in the future by activating the Load button or by clicking on it in the drop-down pattern display.

The alignment of the patterns themselves is not altered when you change the objects by rotating or skewing them for example.

2.7.4   Texture Fill

If you click on the Texture Fill icon in the flyout menu, the dialog window of the same name appears. This window provides more than a hundred bitmap Texture fill patterns, each with its own set of parameters which can be altered to exactly suit your requirements.

A few tips for use when creating texture fills are listed below:

• Because texture fills increase the size of a file, making the printing more time-consuming, it is advisable to

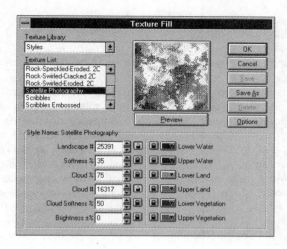

use texture fills only where absolutely necessary.
- A colour monitor produces the best results when you are using texture fills. A monochrome monitor does not display them to their full advantage.
- If you rotate or skew an object containing a texture fill-ing, the filling does not turn along with the object.
- If you change the size of an object containing a filling, the pattern may be deformed. In that case, open the *Texture Fill* dialog window and click on *OK*. You could also open the Fill roll-up menu from the flyout menu and click on the Update From button. Click on the ap-propriate filling and then on the Apply button.

A texture fill is chosen by clicking on its name in the list in the *Texture Fill* dialog window. The preview box shows the basic pattern. Once you have changed the parame-ters, click on the Preview button to view the result.

The left-hand part of the various parameter options con-sists of six numerical parameters. The texture fills have a number between 0 and 32,768 (Texture #). The names of the other parameters depend on the type of texture fill. The various options are largely self-explanatory. A value can be changed by clicking on the arrows or by typing a new value directly in the text box.

The right-hand part of the parameters section contains six colour options which you can alter by clicking on the colour box and choosing a different colour from the drop-down palette. The (colour) options available will depend on the particular texture fill. If you wish to create a colour yourself, or choose a colour by name, click on the More button. When you click on the Preview button, the result of any new specifications will become visible.

2.7.5 PostScript fills

You will only be able to make use of PostScript fills if a PostScript printer is connected to your system. Even then, it is not possible to display them on screen; they are represented symbolically by PSs. The selected patterns are only visible when printed, which might mean that much editorial work may still have to be done.

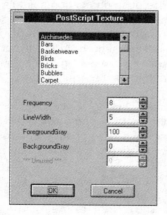

To allocate a PostScript pattern to an object, first click on the PS icon in the flyout menu. The *PostScript Texture* dialog window appears.

This dialog window contains a list of the patterns available. You can also make alterations to the values shown in the lower part of this window to determine the precise printing settings.

Select a pattern from the list and click on *OK*. A selected object (or newly-drawn objects) will then be filled with numerous PSs, indicating that the object has a PostScript filling.

3 CorelDRAW! - Menu commands

In this chapter, we shall deal with the menus and their options. These menu options enable you to implement a large number of commands. The menu bar displays nine menus:

File: This menu contains options for file management, exchange of data with other programs, printing and closing down CorelDRAW!.

Edit: This menu provides typical windows commands for working with graphic objects, such as Cut, Copy, Paste and Delete.

View: Contains commands for specifying the screen display.

Layout: Contains commands for the image layout, such as the page setup and the usage of templates. This menu also provides options for grids and guidelines.

Arrange: Provides options for arranging graphic objects in certain ways, such as aligning, grouping together and combining. This menu also provides options for moving objects to the foreground or background (on different layers).

Effects: Provides options for special graphic effects, such as drawing in perspective, blending from one shape to another and three dimensional display.

Text: Provides options for defining the form and display of texts.

Special: Provides options for specifying preferred settings and for working with patterns.

Help: Provides systematic information about the program and its functions.

The menus will be discussed in detail below and examples will be given to help clarify the information.

The topics in this chapter:

• menu operation
• file management
• importing and exporting objects
• printing images
• editing and managing objects (Cutting, Copying, Pasting etc.)
• applying graphic effects (3D, Blending, Perspective etc.)
• arranging objects (moving to foreground and background)
• creating images at different levels.

The following topics have been dealt with in the section concerning the toolbox, and therefore will only be discussed summarily here:

• text display (see section 2.5.3)
• screen settings (see section 2.1)
• CorelDRAW! preferences (see section 2.1)
• editing objects (see section 2.4).

3.1 Menu operation

The menu names on the menu bar at the top of the screen provide access to the *drop-down* menus. To open a menu, move the mouse pointer to the required name and press the left mouse button; you can also press and hold down the Alt key and then press the underlined letter in the menu name. A menu is closed by clicking anywhere outside the menu or by pressing the Esc key.

Some menu commands or options can be implemented by means of the so-called shortcut key combinations. For example, if you wish to print your work, you can simply press the Ctrl+P key combination instead of opening the *File* menu and choosing *Print*. The Appendix at the back of this book provides an overview of all available shortcut key combinations.

If three dots are shown behind a menu option, this means that a dialog window will appear in which you can make further specifications about how the command is to be executed. All other commands are carried out immediately. Each menu option contains an underlined letter which you can press to activate the option. For instance, when the *File* menu has been opened, you can press the X (the underlined letter in *Exit*) to close down the program.

3.2 The File menu

The *File* menu is subdivided into six groups, providing thirteen options. Options which are related to one another are grouped together. This type of subdivision is also present in all the other menus.

File	
New	Ctrl+N
New From Template...	
Open...	Ctrl+O
Save	Ctrl+S
Save As...	
Import...	
Export...	
Mosaic Roll-Up	Alt+F1
Print...	Ctrl+P
Print Merge...	
Print Setup...	
Color Manager...	
Exit	Alt+F4
1 C:\COREL50\DRAW\BEOWULF.CDR	

The options in the *File* menu enable you to create and manage files, exchange data with other programs, print images, specify colours and close down CorelDRAW!.

At the bottom of the menu, there is a list of the files with which you have most recently worked. Clicking on one of these will open it immediately.

3.2.1 Creating, opening and saving files

The *New*, *New From Template*, *Open*, *Save* and *Save As* options from the *File* menu are used to create and manage images. These functions are described below:

New (Ctrl+N)
This command opens a new worksheet. CorelDRAW! applies the currently active page settings and preferences. If an image is shown on the screen, it will be closed, after you have been given the chance to save it.

New From Template
A template is a collection of styles which, having predefined settings, forms the basis for a new document. This command enables you to use existing templates to create a new drawing. When you select this option, the *New From Template* dialog window appears. Select a template from the list (*.cdt) for the drawing you are about to make. You can apply a style to a selected object by opening the *Layout* menu and selecting *Styles Roll-Up*.

Open (Ctrl+O)
If you wish to begin working with an existing file, click on the *Open* command. The *Open Drawing* dialog window appears.

The figure overleaf shows the drawing when the Options button has been activated. The dialog window has file and directory lists from which you can select the required file, and a preview of the selected file is displayed in the preview window.

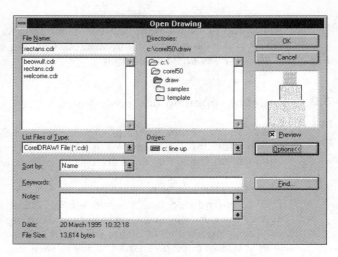

The List Files of Type drop-down list enables you to determine which types of files are to be shown in the file list: CDR (the normal CorelDRAW! graphic files), PAT (pattern file) or CDT (template files). Double click on the required directory to display its contents and click once on the required file to select the image you want to open. Click on *OK* to quit the dialog window.

You can use the other options in this dialog window to look for a certain file or to switch the preview window on or off. Click on the Preview check box to activate or deactivate the preview window.

The Sort By list determines whether the display of the files in the file list is ordered according to name or according to date. The Keywords and Notes boxes display extra information about the images which you recorded in the *Save Drawing* dialog window when you saved the drawing previously.

Save (Ctrl+S)

The *Save* command stores an image on disk(ette). You can keep on working with the image since it also remains in working memory until another image is loaded, or until the program is closed down.

Before an image has been saved, CorelDRAW! always gives it the name UNTITLED.CDR, as shown on the title bar. This name indicates that the drawing has not yet been saved. See section 1.8 for more information about saving files.

Save As

This command saves a drawing under a new name. This refers to both a new drawing and to an existing drawing which you might wish to modify and save under a different name or in a different directory.

When you select this command, the *Save Drawing* dialog window appears in which you must specify the file name, the directory path and the type of file you are saving (with the appropriate extension). In addition, you can also record keywords and notes; this extra information may be useful when browsing through the files later. See also section 1.8.

3.2.2 Managing existing images

The next three options in the *File* menu deal with graphic file management. They make it possible to add images to an existing drawing, prepare currently active images for use in other programs or perform a quick search for certain data. A brief description of these functions is given below:

Import

This option enables you to adopt images and texts from other programs into CorelDRAW!. You can also import other CorelDRAW! files into the currently active drawing.

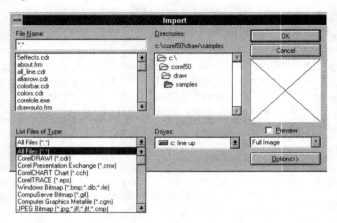

When you have opened the dialog window, specify the type of file you require (List Files of Type), enter the directory path, and type the name in the File Name box or select it from the list if it is displayed there. CorelDRAW! supports forty external file types, so that you can import and edit images and texts from the most common word processors and graphic programs. When you have specified the file you wish to import, click on *OK.* A small box indicates the progress of the importing process. The image subsequently appears in the drawing window. There may be some loss in quality of the image, depending on the file type being imported.

If you click on the Options button in the *Import* dialog window, you can gain additional information about the file being imported.

Export
The *Export* command is used to save an image as an external file type so that it can be imported and edited by a

different program if necessary. You can also do this to only a part of a drawing so that the whole image need not be converted.

Just as with the *Import* command, a dialog window also appears when you select the *Export* command; here too you must specify the drive, the directory path, the file name and the file type. Clicking on *OK* confirms the specifications.

Mosaic Roll-Up (Alt+F1)
This option opens a roll-up menu which displays images in a small preview window. Select the drive and directory containing the required images. The CorelDRAW! images are always automatically displayed first. If you wish to adopt an image into the currently active drawing, select it and drag it to the drawing window.

3.2.3 Print commands

Print (Ctrl+P)
The *Print* command prints the drawing in the drawing window. A dialog window appears in which you can define various default printing options.

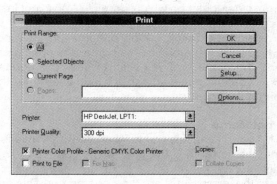

If you only wish to print a part of your drawing, activate the Selected Objects option. Clicking on the Options button enables you to make further, more detailed specifications.

Very large images, which extend beyond the limits of the printable page, can be adjusted to fit on to the page by clicking on the Fit To Page option on the Layout tabsheet. This also applies to very small images which are then enlarged to fill the page.

If you want to print the sections of the drawing which lie outside the printable page on additional pages, activate the Print Tiled Pages option. You also have to activate this option if you have specified a width which exceeds the actual size of the paper in the Width section. Behind Width, you should type the percentage by which the image should be enlarged or reduced.

If you wish to have more than one printed copy, enter the required number in the Copies box in the *Print* dialog window. Instead of printing the file directly, you can print it to a file by activating the Print to File check box. You can then use the file to print the drawing on a printer other than the one presently connected to your system, or from a computer on which CorelDRAW! is not installed.

Pressing the Setup button opens a dialog window in which you can determine the printer, the print orientation and the paper size you wish to use. The normal Windows default print settings are then altered for this one particular occasion.

Print Merge
This option enables you to insert varying sections of text into the currently active image. The corresponding number of versions (in other words, the fixed image along with the varying text) are then printed out. This option is

similar to the form letter function in a word processing program. The image is created, and space is reserved for the text. This text is stored as a special file type, and is then adopted into the image.

You should not use this option when the varying text has special features such as blended or three-dimensional text, text which is aligned to a certain object or text in which certain character attributes have been altered. You should create the text in the Windows Notebook or in another text editor which is capable of saving it as 'pure' ASCII text.

Print Setup

Activate the Print Setup option to select the printer and to define the print settings you wish to use to print the drawing. The *Print Setup* dialog window appears.

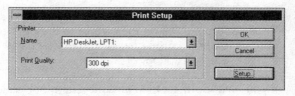

Specify the relevant printer in the Name text box. This will normally be the printer you installed for all your Windows programs. The drop-down list will only show connected devices or previously-defined printers. Any other printers can only be installed by means of the Control Panel in Windows.

Click on the Setup button to open the dialog window which corresponds to the defined printer. The options provided will depend on the printer in question. The window will look something like the one shown overleaf.

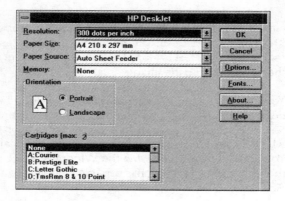

The Orientation section determines the way in which the page is to be printed, Portrait (vertically) or Landscape (horizontally). This setting should correspond to that in the *Page Setup* dialog window (*Layout* menu).

As you see, you can specify the Paper Size and the Paper Source. Click on the arrows to the right of these options to open a drop-down list from which you can select the required option.

If you click on the Options button, another dialog window appears in which you can define further settings for the selected printer. Click on the Help button if you wish more information about these.

3.2.4 Colour display

Color Manager

The Color Manager enables you to create a so-called colour profile based on the available monitor, scanner and printer. These specifications assist CorelDRAW! in producing a high-fidelity colour display when different monitors, printers or scanners are being used.

Using this customised profile, you can ensure that:

* the colours on the screen correspond as much as possible to those on the printer;
* the images and colours in your drawing are repro-duced by the printer as reliably as possible;
* the colours generated by the scanner correspond as closely as possible to the original version.

The default settings provided in this dialog window have been tested extensively, so it is advisable to use these where appropriate.

3.2.5   Closing down CorelDRAW!

Exit (Alt+F4)
The *Exit* command closes down the CorelDRAW! pro-gram. If you have not saved (the most recent version of) your work, you will be given the chance to do so before the program is closed down.

The next time that you open CorelDRAW!, the program applies the same settings as those used in the previous session.

3.2.6   Quick file access

1, 2, 3, 4
If you have saved files previously, the four of these which you last edited are listed at the bottom of the *File* menu. Clicking on any one of these will open it immediately. This method is thus quicker than using the *Open* com-mand.

3.3 The Edit menu

This menu is subdivided into five groups, providing a total of fifteen options.

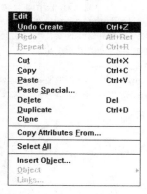

3.3.1 Reversing and repeating commands

The first group in the *Edit* menu provides an opportunity to undo the previous action, to redo it again if you have second thoughts, and to repeat the previous action.

Undo (Ctrl+Z)

The last performed action can be undone by selecting this option. It should be activated immediately after the action has been carried out, otherwise undoing that specific action will no longer be possible. There are also several actions which cannot be undone by means of this command:

- changing the screen display, such as enlarging or reducing
- file management actions such as Opening, Saving and Importing
- selection actions, such as node selection.

Redo (Alt+Ret)

Immediately you have undone an action, the *Redo* option becomes available. You can then simply redo the action you have just undone. Pressing the key combination Alt+Ret (Alt+Enter) is a quick and easy method of implementing this action.

Repeat (Ctrl+R)

The *Repeat* command repeats the previous command or action whenever possible. Use this option when you wish to successively enlarge, reduce or rotate a number of objects for example.

3.3.2 Exchanging, copying and deleting data

The following four commands are available in all Windows applications. They enable the user to exchange and copy data by means of the Clipboard.

Cut (Ctrl+X)

The *Cut* command removes the selected object from the drawing window and stores it on the Clipboard in Windows. You can subsequently paste the contents of the Clipboard to a different CorelDRAW! file or to a file in a different Windows application.

Copy (Ctrl+C)

The *Copy* command has much the same effect as the *Cut* command, but a copy of the object is stored on the Clipboard; the original remains in the drawing window. You can paste the contents of the Clipboard to other files.

Paste (Ctrl+V)

The *Paste* command inserts the contents of the Clipboard into the currently active Windows application file if the file type is supported. CorelDRAW! supports the pasting of vector and pixel-based images and also text. Accordingly, a flexible exchange of data with other Windows applications is possible.

Paste Special

The *Paste Special* command enables you to create an OLE connection with other Windows applications, by means of the Clipboard. For instance: Imagine you have created a diagram using CorelCHART and you wish to give it special graphic features using CorelDRAW!. Select the chart by clicking on it, open the *Edit* menu and select *Copy Chart*. The diagram is copied to the *Clipboard* and you can then close down CorelCHART if you wish. Switch to, or start up CorelDRAW! and open the *Edit* menu. Select *Paste Special*. The corresponding dialog window appears.

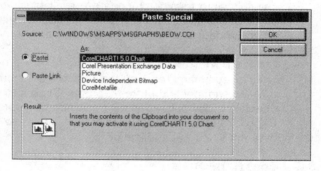

Select the line 'CorelCHART! 5.0 Chart' and click on the Paste option button. The chart is then automatically inserted into CorelDRAW!. You can make alterations to the chart using the functions available in CorelCHART by simply double clicking on the chart. CorelCHART is started up by means of the OLE connection and you can make use of its functions to edit the chart.

Delete (Del)

The *Delete* command enables you to remove a selected object. If no action is carried out immediately afterwards, it is possible to recall the deleted object by means of the *Undo* command.

Duplicate (Ctrl+D)

The *Duplicate* command enables you to copy selected objects in the drawing window. This is done directly, not via the Clipboard. The *Preferences* option from the *Special* menu enables you to specify where duplicates and clones are to be placed.

Clone

This command copies the selected object and inserts it next to the original with a small space inbetween. Most actions which are performed upon the original are automatically passed on to the clone. For example, if the filling in the original is altered, the clone also acquires the new filling. If you change a feature of the clone, that feature of the clone is no longer dependent on the original. Any changes to the original with respect to that feature have no effect upon the clone. When you have stretched a clone for example, any alterations to the shape of the original will not be applied to the clone.

3.3.3 Object attributes

Copy Attributes From

This option enables you to copy the attributes from one selected object to another object. When you click on this option, the *Copy Attributes* dialog window appears in which you can specify which attributes you wish to copy:

* Outline Pen
* Outline Color

- Fill
- Text Attributes.

We shall use a text to illustrate this. Text attributes such as font, point size and spacing can be transferred to a different text or section of text. Horizontal and vertical character shifts and the angle of placement (all these options are to be found in the *Character Attributes* dialog window under the *Text* menu) cannot be transferred. Proceed as follows to copy text attributes:

1) Select the text whose attributes you wish to change.
2) Open the *Edit* menu and select *Copy Attributes From*.
3) Activate the Text Attributes check box.
4) Click on OK. The mouse pointer changes into a thick black arrow.
5) Click on the text whose attributes are to be copied to the selected text.

3.3.4 Selecting objects

Select All
This option selects all the objects in the current drawing. This also applies to objects which are not displayed on the present screen or lie outside the printable page. The command which you now choose will be applied to all the objects in the drawing.

3.3.5 Objects from other applications

The commands in this group are used to insert objects from other programs (texts, tables, images etc.) into a CorelDRAW! drawing.

Insert Object
This option enables you to adopt an object created in a different application into the current drawing. In this way,

you can insert a CorelCHART diagram, a Microsoft Excel worksheet or a Paintbrush drawing into the Corel-DRAW! drawing window.

When you click on this option, a dialog window appears displaying a list of all programs with which CorelDRAW! is able to exchange data. If you wish to create a new object, ensure that the Create New option button is activated. Select the required program and click on the OK button or double click on the name of the program to open it. This program appears on the screen in front of the currently active application, in our case Corel-DRAW!. Create the object and then close down the application. The newly-created object is inserted into the CorelDRAW! drawing. If you wish to make use of an existing object, activate the Create from File option button in the *Insert Object* dialog box. Then specify the path and file name in the File text box, or click on the Browse button to select a file from the subsequent list. The object is inserted into the CorelDRAW! drawing. If you wish to edit the object using the functions available in the source application, double click on the object. It can be useful to save any newly created object for later use. If you activate the Link check box in the *Insert Object* dialog window, the inserted object will be updated when the source file is altered.

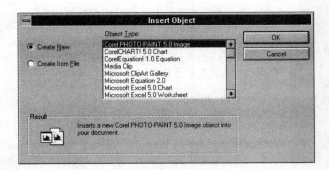

141

In this way, you can spread a number of objects through-out various Windows applications.
You can also, of course, adopt CorelDRAW! drawings into word processors and spreadsheets.

Object...Edit/Open

This option opens the application in which the selected embedded object was created. You can then edit the object. When you have made the modifications and have closed the application, the altered object is adopted into the CorelDRAW! file. The exact name of the command depends on the application used to create the object in question. For instance, if the object was created in Microsoft Excel, the menu will show *Spreadsheet Object*.

Links

If you have created links between objects (in the *Insert Object* dialog window for instance), you can activate the *Links* option to update, change or break the links. This can be done to each individual OLE link. The list shows internal links between CorelDRAW! files and also external links to other Windows applications such as Word for Windows for example.

3.4 The View menu

The functions used in CorelDRAW! to help design objects were dealt with in detail in the first two chapters: the Rulers, colour palettes, preview windows and roll-up menus. Accordingly, we shall give a brief summary of the options available in the *View* menu.

3.4.1 Screen utilities

Rulers

Select this option to display or hide the horizontal and vertical Rulers. The Rulers enable you to determine the size and position of objects accurately.

Toolbox

This option enables you to specify whether or not the toolbox should be visible and whether or not it should be movable.

Color Palette

This command opens a submenu with options providing various colour palettes: None, Uniform Colors, Custom Colors, FOCOLTONE Colors, PANTONE Spot Colors, PANTONE Process Colors and TRUMATCH Colors.

Roll-Ups

This option opens the *Roll-Ups* dialog window, in which you can open and arrange roll-up menus on the screen. All the available roll-up menus are shown in the list, and the currently activated roll-up menus are indicated by a small icon to the left of the name. If you wish to show a roll-up menu, click on its name in the list, and place a cross in the appropriate check box to make it visible, to arrange it on the screen and/or to display it opened (Rolled Down). You can select a number of roll-up menus at once by holding down the Ctrl key while clicking.

3.4.2   Display modes

Wireframe (Shift+F9)

The Wireframe option switches back and forth between the normal view and the wireframe model display mode. A drawing can be edited more quickly in the wireframe mode since only the outline is redrawn with each alteration. Pressing the Shift+F9 key combination is quicker than selecting this option from the *View* menu; you can also click on the Wireframe button on the toolbar along the top of the screen.

Bitmaps

This option enables you to activate and deactivate the display of bitmaps (e.g. imported BMP files from Windows) in the drawing window. If you are working in the Wireframe view, deactivating the bitmap display (no tick next to Visible in the submenu) will considerably speed up the speed at which the screen is redrawn. In that case, only the frame of the bitmap is shown. In the normal display, bitmaps are always fully shown (there is always a tick next to the Visible option).

Color Correction

This option enables you to improve the colour display. However, redrawing bitmaps does become more time-consuming.

3.4.3 Displaying objects

Full-Screen Preview (F9)

This option shows the drawing or the selected objects on the entire screen, without any other screen elements being displayed. Press any key to restore the normal screen display.

Preview Selected Only

When you activate this option, only the selected object is shown when the Full-Screen Preview is activated (F9).

3.4.4 Redrawing the window

Refresh Window (Ctrl+W)

This option redraws the objects on the screen. It is used chiefly to remove residues of previous drawings, or to continue the redrawing process after a pause.

3.5   The Layout menu

The options in the *Layout* menu enable you to determine the page settings, the layers and styles to be used in a drawing, and the usage of grids and guidelines.

3.5.1   Inserting and deleting pages, the page setup

Insert Page
If you require an extra page for a drawing, select this option. A dialog window appears in which you can specify the number of pages required and where they should be inserted (Before or After the current page).

Delete Page
If you select this option, you can specify the number of pages you wish to delete by typing the first and last pages to be deleted.

Go To Page
If you wish to switch to another page in a document which contains several pages, select this option from the *Layout* menu. You can also click on the small arrows at the extreme left of the horizontal scroll bar at the bottom of the screen.

Page Setup
Activating this option opens the *Page Setup* dialog window in which you can specify the page size, layout and display. The various possibilities provided by the three tabsheets have been dealt with in detail in section 2.1.1. Note that:

• When you save a drawing, the relevant page settings are also saved.
• The settings influence the size of the printable page.
• The chosen paper size must correspond to that in the

Print Setup dialog window (via *File* menu and Setup button).

3.5.2 Layers and styles

CorelDRAW! makes a distinction between images at different levels, which makes it possible, just as with film effects, to work with separate *layers*. It is advisable to use this technique when several independent picture areas have to be drawn and superimposed. The more complex a total image is, the more difficult it is to distinguish between the separate objects which make up the image, and therefore the more difficult it is to select certain components when necessary. Especially in the Wireframe View, it is almost impossible to see which lines are in the *foreground* and which are in the *background*.

Up until now, we have created drawings in CorelDRAW! on a single layer. But you can also create drawings consisting of several layers so that the objects are placed on top of one another. In that case, with two objects, the result can be as follows:

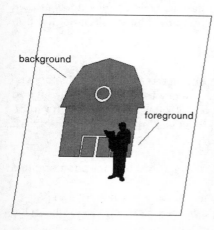

There are two objects which overlap one another. One is in the foreground, the other is in the background and is partially covered by the first object. It is important to keep this in mind when working with CorelDRAW!: objects are not changed or erased by other objects, they are only covered.

Imagine that a second layer is placed over the first one.

You can also place various overlapping objects on this second layer. The combination of these two layers could look something like this:

The advantage of this is that you can experiment on the second layer without running the risk of accidentally altering the images on the first layer. In this way, you can make the basic elements of the drawings on the first layer and experiment with variations on the second layer. CorelDRAW! enables you to make use of as many layers as you like. It is advisable to use these when working with complex drawings.

Layers Roll-Up

If you wish to create a new layer, open the *Layout* menu and select *Layers Roll-Up*. A small roll-up menu appears. Click on the small arrow pointing to the right. Another menu is displayed in which you can create new layers or edit or delete existing ones. You can also move or copy objects to a different layer.

Click on the *New* command. The *New Layer* dialog window appears. You can now make specifications for the

new layer. The Visible option determines whether or not
the layer should be visible. The Printable option determines whether or not the layer should be printed. If you
activate the Locked option, it will not be possible to alter
objects on this layer; use this option when parts of an image should be protected. The Color Override option
makes it possible to recognise objects which are on a
particular layer in a complex drawing. Each object on a
layer is displayed as a transparent wireframe model. This
is done in the selected colour which has been assigned
to the layer. This option does not change the outline and
filling of the object; it only affects the screen display
when you are working in the editable preview mode.

You can edit all objects on all layers regardless of the
layer which has been activated. The Locked option, if activated, remains in force.

If you have created various layers and wish to activate a
certain one, click once on the required layer in the roll-
up menu. If you double click on the name in the roll-up
menu, you can change the specifications you have made
for that layer.

Styles Roll-Up
You may wish to apply certain features of an object to another object. For instance, you may wish to apply the formatting created for a square to a circle.

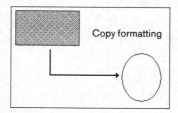

Copy formatting

If you often make use of certain features or formatting,
you can save them as a *style*. To do so, click with the

right mouse button on the object whose formatting you wish to preserve. If you have already allocated a different function to the right mouse button, press and hold it down until the *Object Menu* appears (see section 2.1.4). Select *Save As Style* from this menu.

The *Save As Style* dialog window appears. Type a name (maximum 15 characters) in the text box. There are three distinct sorts of styles: for artistic text, for paragraph text and for graphic objects. CorelDRAW! recognises these styles automatically. The relevant features appear in the dialog window. Specify which features you wish to save by clicking on the appropriate check boxes. Click on OK to confirm your selection.

The style is then adopted into the *Styles* roll-up menu, from which you can apply it to other objects. To do this, select the required object and then open the *Styles* roll-up menu from the *Layout* menu. You can also use the Ctrl+F5 shortcut key combination.

Click on the required style in the roll-up menu and click on the Apply button. The buttons at the top of the roll-up menu enable you to activate and deactivate the display of the different sorts of styles. You can also apply a style by clicking on an object with the right mouse button to produce the *Object Menu* and then selecting the *Apply Style* option.

3.5.3 Grid and guidelines

The other options in the *Layout* menu concern placing objects at certain positions on the screen.

Grid & Scale Setup

This option determines the grid origin, the distance between the grid lines, the grid display and the scale. Keep the following points in mind:

- The grid settings are saved along with the drawing.
- When you change the grid frequency, the position of objects in the drawing is not changed.
- If you change the units of measurement for the grid frequency, the values in the text box are not altered. You have to specify any new values here yourself.

See section 2.1.2 for more information about this dialog window.

Guidelines Setup

You can make use of this option to display, move or delete the guidelines you use to help you place objects at required positions. You can also insert, move or delete guidelines by dragging them to, or out of, the Ruler.

3.5.4 Automatic alignment

The last three options in the *Layout* menu concern aligning objects precisely.

Snap to Grid (Ctrl+Y)
This option determines that objects which are nearby a
gridline are automatically drawn, from a certain point on-
wards, to the line. This principle also applies to the other
options in this section. If this *snap* function is activated, it
is much easier to position objects adjacent to one another. This also enables you to draw objects to a required size. The grid is not printed. (See section 2.1.2 for
more information.)

Snap to Guidelines
This option, like the *Snap to Grid* option, places objects
at certain positions automatically; in this case they are
drawn to the specified guidelines. You can place any
number of guidelines in the drawing window.

Snap to Objects
This option places drawn objects next to other existing
objects in a drawing. This option has priority over the
other two *snap* options. If all three are on, an object being moved will snap to the nearest stationary object regardless of the proximity of grid and guidelines.

3.6 The Arrange menu

The *Arrange* menu provides options for organising one
or more objects in a certain way. Most options deal with
the mutual relationship between objects.

3.6.1 Placing the objects

Align

If you wish to place several objects exactly next to or under one another, select the *Align* option from the *Arrange* menu.

If you want to align a number of objects to one object, hold down the Shift key while clicking on the objects to be aligned. Make sure that the object to which they are to be aligned is the last one chosen. Then open the *Arrange* menu and select *Align*. Specify the required alignment for the objects by placing a cross in the Vertical and/or Horizontal sections.

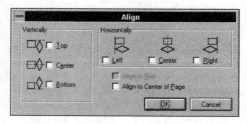

Order

In section 3.5.2, we discussed the fact that each layer has a foreground and a background. Have a look at the figure below:

A man is situated in the background. There is a wall in front of him and there is a tree in the foreground. There are thus three levels. Each new object has been created in front of the other existing objects. Therefore, to make this picture, the man would be drawn first, then the wall and then the tree. If you wish to change this order, proceed as follows:

1) Select the object that you want to relocate.
2) Open the *Arrange* menu and select *Order*. Choose the required option from the subsequent submenu.

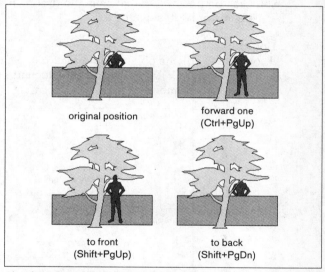

original position

forward one
(Ctrl+PgUp)

to front
(Shift+PgUp)

to back
(Shift+PgDn)

3) In our example, we have chosen the *Forward One* option (shortcut key Ctrl+PgUp) to move the man.

The *To Front* and *To Back* options enable you to move an object to the foreground or the background in one go.

3.6.2   Grouping objects

Group

It is possible to combine various objects to form a single object. This provides the advantage that several drawn objects can be selected with one click and then edited. In that case, you could, for example, specify the fill colour, the line thickness or the line colour quite easily.

Grouping objects is carried out by first selecting all the objects which are to belong to the group. Then open the *Arrange* menu and select *Group*. Subsequently, when you click on one of the objects in the group, all the others are immediately selected too.

Ungroup

If you wish to edit the objects individually once more, you can reverse the *Group* command by selecting *Ungroup* from the *Arrange* menu.

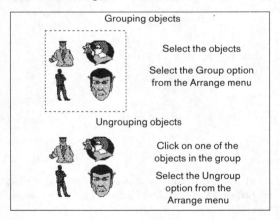

Grouping objects

Select the objects

Select the Group option
from the Arrange menu

Ungrouping objects

Click on one of the
objects in the group

Select the Ungroup
option from the
Arrange menu

3.6.3   Combining objects

Objects can not only be grouped, they can also be combined. The difference is that combined objects can also be edited using the Shape tool. In addition, transparent objects can be created. If two overlapping objects are present, it is possible to see through the one in the fore-ground.

In the figure, Charlie Chaplin is standing behind the harp. If the objects were not com-bined, the inner part of the harp would not be transparent. A closed area with black lines would be displayed. The fol-lowing example makes it even more clear:

The slogan in the background is partially covered by the stripe in the foreground. After combination, the letters shine through.

Select all the objects which are to be combined. Then open the Arrange menu and select Combine.

Break Apart
Select the *Break Apart* option to reverse the *Combine* command.

Weld

If you want to 'physically' join overlapping objects to form a single object with a common outline, you should use the *Weld* option from the *Arrange* menu. First select the objects to be welded and then apply the command. The selected objects are joined to form a single object and the points of intersection of the objects are then removed. The welded object assumes the outline and the filling of the object that was last selected. If you select the objects using the marquee frame, the welded object is assigned the outline and filling of the lowest object on the screen.

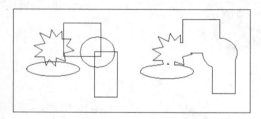

Intersection

If you want to cut a new object out of a number of overlapping objects, open the *Arrange* menu and select *Intersection*. The entire procedure is as follows: Select the objects which overlap by clicking on them while holding down the Shift key or by dragging a marquee frame over them. Open the *Arrange* menu and select *Intersection*. A new object is created that assumes the shape of the overlapping area.

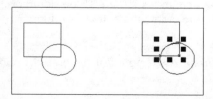

Trim

If you wish to remove the overlapping area completely, select the overlapping objects first, making sure that the object that is to be trimmed is selected last. Then select *Trim* from the *Arrange* menu. The last selected object is trimmed according to the shape of the overlapping object(s). The effect only becomes visible when you move the objects away from one another.

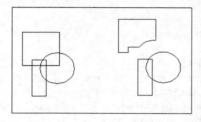

3.6.4 Separating objects and converting to curves

Separate

Objects which formed the basis of new shapes by means of the *Blend*, the *Contour* and the *Extrude* roll-up menus (*Effects* menu), can be separated again using the *Separate* command from the *Arrange* menu. It will also separate text from the path to which it has been fitted using the *Fit Text to Path* command (*Text* menu) and from the object to which it has been aligned using the *Snap to Object* command (*Layout* menu).

Convert to Curves

If your drawing contains closed objects or curves whose form you wish to alter, you should first convert these to curves. You can edit them using the Shape tool.

3.7 The Effects menu

There are three groups of commands in the *Effects* menu for applying graphic effects. These enable you to make transformations, edit the contours, create perspective, create blends and display objects with three-dimensional effects. We shall restrict our description to the basic functions here.

3.7.1 Transforming objects

Transform Roll-Up
If you want to move, rotate, skew, stretch and mirror objects, you can open the *Transform* roll-up menu. This provides a number of options which you can use to make exact specifications concerning how the object is to be transformed.

The facilities provided here correspond to those provided by the Pick tool (see chapter 1), except for the fact that the Pick tool does not allow you to make such exact specifications.

Clear Transformations
This CorelDRAW! function enables you to restore the original form of the object prior to the transformation. Accordingly, you can try out a number of transformations before deciding which one to keep.

3.7.2   Advanced functions for manipulating objects

The *Effects* menu provides some of CorelDRAW!'s most sophisticated commands for editing objects.

Add Perspective
Placing objects in perspective helps give objects a three-dimensional effect. We shall use a simple blocked grid to demonstrate this.

The left figure displays a two-dimensional board. The right-hand figure shows this board when the perspective has been shifted. A spatial effect has been created. To apply this spatial effect, proceed as follows:

1)   Select the object, open the *Effects* menu and select *Add Perspective*.
2)   Click on one of the four corners, hold down the mouse button and drag the frame to the required position. When you have the right perspective, release the mouse button.
3)   You can repeat this procedure with the other corners until you have produced the desired result.

Note
The perspective effect will not be shown with fillings, which are always adjusted to fill any shapes. The effects apply to objects (lines, rectangles, ellipses etc.) which have been combined (by means of the *Group*, *Combine*

or *Weld* commands from the *Arrange* menu if necessary) to form a unit.

The display in perspective seems to place some parts of
the figure in the distance. In other words, all straight
lines in the object are directed towards a vanishing
point. This point is indicated by a cross in CorelDRAW!.
You can also drag this cross to alter the perspective.
When you drag an object in a horizontal and vertical direction, two vanishing points appear which you can position independently.

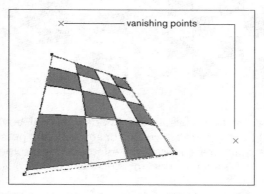

Objects which have been given perspective can be restored to their original shapes by selecting the *Clear
Perspective* command from the lower part of the *Effects*
menu.

Just as with other modifications, you can copy perspec-
tives from one object to another. This is done by means
of the *Copy* command from the *Effects* menu. Select
Perspective From in the subsequent submenu.

Envelope Roll-Up
This option enables you to modify the contours of objects in CorelDRAW!. You can regard the contour as be-

ing an elastic border which you can pull in any desired direction. The objects within the contour are also pulled in this direction.

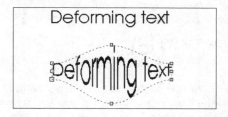

To work with this option, you first have to select the object in question. Then open the *Effects* menu and select *Envelope Roll-Up*.

The central part of the menu contains four options for making a contour. To apply a new contour, first click on the Add New button and then choose one of the forms. The selected object is displayed in a frame, resembling that which we previously saw with the Shape tool. The difference is that you can now alter entire shapes and not only separate parts. The dotted frame has a number of handles which you can drag to give the contour a new form. Drag the handles and then click on the Apply button. The figure overleaf shows examples of the various contour forms.

The Reset Envelope button undoes any changes to the envelope since it was last applied. If you add a new envelope without applying it, Reset Envelope will remove it. If you wish to undo the changes to the contour, open the *Edit* menu and select *Undo*.

The Create From button can also be very useful. It enables you to apply a created envelope to another object. First select the object which is to receive the new contour. The mouse pointer then changes into a thick black arrow. Click on the object whose contour you wish to copy.

The Add Preset button enables you to apply other forms of contours to the selected object. You can then edit these further if required.

Blend Roll-Up

Blending one object into another can provide interesting effects, as the next figure demonstrates.

Blending has taken place between two separate objects. A kind of metamorphose has occurred.

To blend two objects, proceed as follows:

1) Select both objects by holding down the Shift key and clicking.
2) Open the *Effect* menu and select *Blend Roll-Up*. The roll-up menu appears.

3) Specify the number of steps and the amount of rotation which are to be applied in the blending.
4) Start the procedure by clicking on Apply.

If you blend objects with different colour filling, it is possible to specify the course of the colour blending. Click on the button showing the circle in the *Blend* roll-up menu. A larger colour circle appears containing a black line. This line indicates the starting and end colour of the blending process. If you click on the Rainbow check box, the black line will move to the outer rim of the circle. If you click on the buttons under this option, you can specify whether the line is to take the long way round the circle, in other words, flow through as many colours as possible, or the short way round.

But the blend can also take place along a specified line. To do this, click on the Freehand tool and draw a line between the two objects. Then select the two objects using the Shift key and open the *Blend* roll-up menu. Click on the curved line icon at the bottom of the menu and then on the New Path option. A thick black arrow appears. Move this arrow to the freehand line you drew between the objects and click on it. The line is activated. Click on the Apply button. The objects are blended into one another along the given route.

If you also activate the Rotate All option, the objects are rotated to conform to the slope of the path.

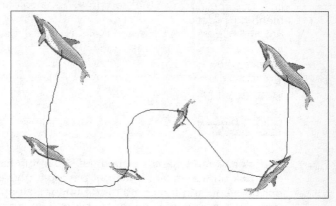

You can remove the blending by opening the *Effects* menu and selecting the *Clear Blend* option. The two original objects remain.

Extrude Roll-Up

You can easily create three-dimensional and perspective effects in CorelDRAW! drawings.

This is done as follows. First create a two-dimensional object, a coloured square for example. Then open the *Ef-*

fects menu and select *Extrude Roll-Up*. The roll-up menu appears:

A dotted frame appears around the square (if this is not so, click on the square button at the top of the *Extrude* roll-up menu and then on the Edit button), along with a cross in the square. Drag the cross to the middle of the square. Type the number 50 in the Depth box. The screen should look like this:

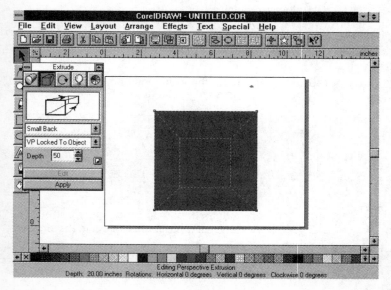

Then click on the Apply button. It seems as if nothing has changed but we have just created a three-dimensional square, viewed from the front (small at the back) . By placing the cross to the middle, you have moved the vanishing point to the back, simultaneously creating a front surface. This can be demonstrated quite easily. Click on the middle button with the circle and the arrow. A round, three-dimensional ball appears in the *Extrude* roll-up menu.

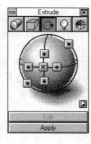 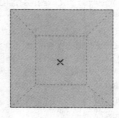

Click on the directional arrows in the *Extrude* figure. The three-dimensional figure turns in the drawing window.

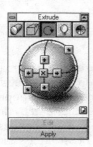 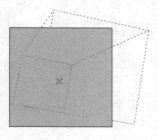

When you are satisfied, click on the Apply button. The perspective is now assigned to the object in the drawing window.

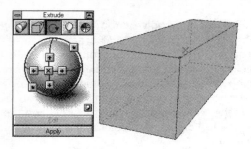

You have now added dimension and perspective to the object, but it still looks a little simple. We shall give it a bit more body. Click on the button showing the lightbulb in the *Extrude* roll-up menu and then on one of the numbered buttons. A cube now appears enclosing the ball.

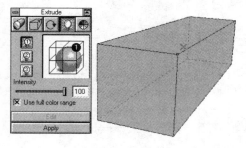

The button you clicked on represents the primary light source. Now place this light source at the required point in the cube by dragging the number to the appropriate position. The light intensity can be changed by dragging the small bar along the scale. The value changes correspondingly. You can also place other light sources by clicking on the button and dragging the number to the required position in the cube. Their intensity can be changed on the scale as described. Click on Apply to bring the specifications into force.

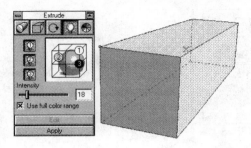

It is, however, easier to work with the first button in the *Extrude* roll-up menu. When you activate it, you can select one of the options in the drop-down list. You only need to make a choice and then click on the Apply button. The object in the drawing window is then assigned a preset three-dimensional effect.

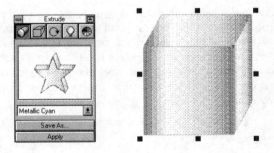

You can remove the three-dimensional effects by opening the *Effects* menu and selecting *Clear Extrude*.

Contour Roll-Up
The *Contour* roll-up menu also enables you to give objects spatial effects. Examine the figure below. In all three cases, a white circle of the same size was the point of departure.

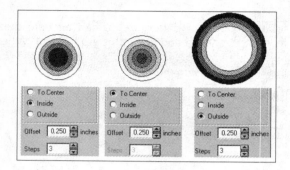

The application of contours to text objects gives an effect similar to that provided by blending, but in this case, only individual objects can be treated. In addition, it is not possible to blend along a specified line. Nevertheless, it is possible to create realistic effects.

First select the objects whose contours you wish to modify. Open the *Effects* menu and select *Contour Roll-Up*. Click on the required amount of steps to specify the blending appearance. Specify the thickness of the contours in the Offset section and choose the colours for the Outline and the Fill from the corresponding drop-down palettes.

PowerLine Roll-Up

The *PowerLine* roll-up menu enables you to create classic effects, such as calligraphic penstrokes, airbrush effects or woodcut patterns. You can allocate these effects both prior to and after drawing the line. When you select the *PowerLine Roll-Up* option from the *Effects* menu, the following menu appears:

The drop-down options list provides 24 different standard settings. When you click on one of these, a preview appears in the sample box in the roll-up menu. In the Max. Width box, you determine the maximum width the drawn lines may assume. If the Apply when drawing lines option is active, you can assign the specified features to the lines you subsequently draw. The buttons along the top of the roll-up menu enable you to choose a predefined pen style, specify the nib shape and intensity, and regulate the speed and ink flow with which the line is drawn.

Click on the middle button to determine the pen-nib shape by means of the Angle, Nib Ratio and Intensity value boxes. If these options are not shown in the roll-up menu, click on the small page symbol next to Nib Shape. You can also directly change the shape of the pen-nib in the sample box. Click on the box, hold down the mouse button and drag the shape in the box.

The third button along the top determines the shape of the line at bends and how the lines come to an end. Speed regulates the width at points where the line changes direction; the more angular the change, the more pronounced the effect. Spread acts as a smoothness control; the greater the value, the smoother the line. Ink Flow determines the amount of ink in the pen, as it were. The lower the value, the less the coverage as the line becomes thinner.

You can save the settings you specify for use later by clicking on the Save As button and giving the style a name.

Lens Roll-Up

The *Lens* roll-up menu enables you to alter sections of an image, by enlargement, or a colour filter, inverse video effect etc.

To try out this function, type the text 'The Lens Effect' using the Artistic Text tool. Then draw a circle or ellipse using the Ellipse tool, making sure that it has no filling. Select the circle and drag it to cover a part of the text. Open the *Effects* menu, select *Lens Roll-Up* and activate Magnify from the drop-down list. Click on the Apply button. The text under the lens is magnified.

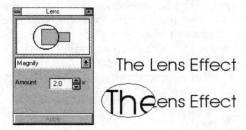

This roll-up menu provides additional possibilities to display an object in another way. You can make it clearer for instance by selecting Brighten and specifying the required amount of light. Try out the various possibilities from the list before deciding definitely.

PowerClip
If you wish to join two objects together so that one object is integrated into the other, select *PowerClip* from the *Effects* menu.

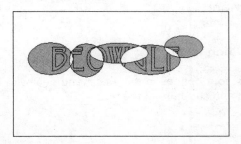

The background object is called the container. To insert an object into a container, first select the object to be inserted. Then open the *Effects* menu and select *Power-Clip*. Select *Place Inside Container* from the submenu which appears. The mouse pointer changes into a thick arrow. Use this arrow to click on the object which is to be the container. The selected object is then integrated. If you wish to alter the position of this object, select the *PowerClip* command once again and then *Edit Contents* from the submenu. You can move, enlarge and reduce, rotate, stretch and shrink the object. The *Finishing Editing This Level* option concludes the editing process.

Clear Effect

As mentioned, you can clear the effect you have just applied by selecting this option.

Copy and Clone

The effects discussed in this chapter can also be applied to other existing objects. This is done by selecting the *Copy* or *Clone* command from the *Effects* menu. If you clone an effect, any alterations to the original object are also passed on to the clone. This is referred to as a server/client or master/client relationship.

3.8 Text menu

3.8.1 Formatting text

The first four options in the *Text* menu deal with the formatting and structure of the text.

Text Roll-Up

This option opens the roll-up menu of the same name, enabling you to apply text and formatting features quickly and easily.

If no object is selected when you make changes in the *Text* roll-up menu, the changes you make will become the default settings for paragraph and artistic text. The shortcut key combination for this option is Ctrl+F2.

The other options from the first group enable you to define attributes for the corresponding text types and sections of text.

Character (Ctrl+T)

The *Character* option opens the *Character Attributes* dialog window in which you can choose the font, the font size and the style for the selected text.

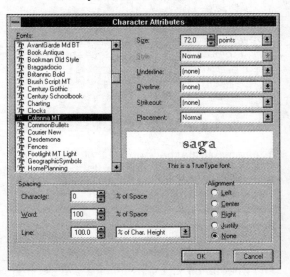

You can alter the attributes of the individual characters by dragging the cursor across them or by selecting them using the Shape tool. If you use the Shape tool, you can rotate and move the characters horizontally and vertically.

Paragraph

If you select the *Paragraph* option, a dialog window is opened in which you can define the spacing, tabs, indents and bullets for a text.

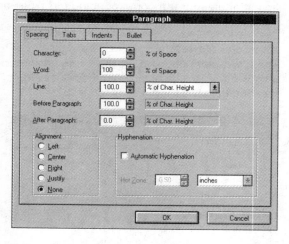

You can activate the various tabsheets in the *Paragraph* dialog window by clicking on the tabs along the top of the window.

Frame

The *Frame* option formats the selected paragraph text into column layout, as in a newspaper for example. You define whether or not the columns are to be of equal width, and also the space between the columns. This option is not available for artistic text.

3.8.2 Aligning text

You can obtain special effects by aligning text to an object or to a specified line.

Fit Text To Path
If you wish to align a text to an object, proceed as follows:

1) Create an artistic text and an object, such as a circle, to which you wish to align the text.
2) Select the text then press and hold down the Shift key. Select the object.
3) Open the *Text* menu and select *Fit Text To Path*, or press the shortcut key combination Ctrl+F. Keep in mind that only artistic text can be aligned to an object.

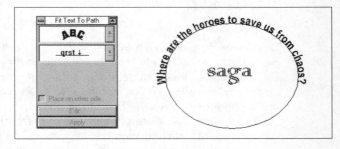

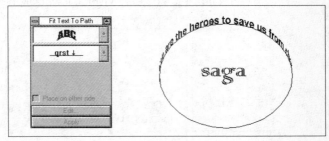

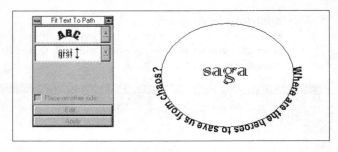

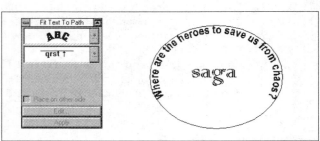

The upper drop-down list in the *Fit Text To Path* roll-up menu determines the alignment of the text to the object. The lower drop-down list determines the distance to the object and the display. For instance, you can place the text on under or above the line of the object. The Place On Other Side check box enables you to mirror the text. When you are satisfied with the alignment of the text, you can remove the object to which it was aligned.

Align Text to Baseline

You can also align text to its own baseline, in other words, the imaginary line along which the text characters are placed.

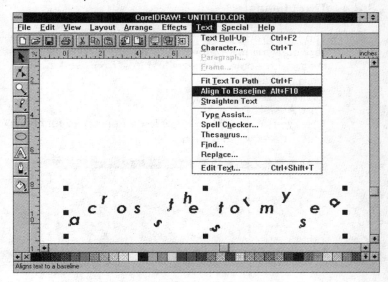

This action does not affect character angle or horizontal spacing. When the text has been aligned to the baseline, it will look like this:

Straighten Text

If you select the *Straighten Text* option, the text is completely straightened out on the baseline. Horizontal and vertical shifts are removed and angles are brought back to zero, although the specified character spacing remains.

a c r o s s t h e s t o r m y s e a

3.8.4 Text utilities

The next group of options provides features which are very convenient when working with text. You may be familiar with some of these features from working with word processors.

Type Assist

The *Type Assist* option provides a number of functions which make typing easier.

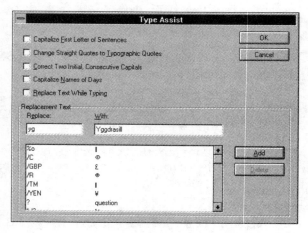

You can, for example, replace an abbreviation automatically with the proper word. This can be very useful if you wish to enter text containing long words, especially if you have to do so repeatedly. For instance, instead of typing 'Self-centred unscrupulous ministers' you could simply type 'scum'. Click on the Add button and CorelDRAW! automatically places the correct word in the text. Further in this dialog window, you can ensure that each sentence begins with a capital letter and you can have normal, straight quotation marks converted to typographic ones.

If the Replace Text While Typing check box is activated, CorelDRAW! will enter the specified text while you are typing.

Spell Checker

A text with spelling mistakes gives your presentation a clumsy appearance. However, it is difficult to avoid these, especially in lengthy texts. CorelDRAW! provides a function to check texts, the Spell Checker. Select the text in question, open the *Text* menu and select *Spell Check*. A dialog window appears.

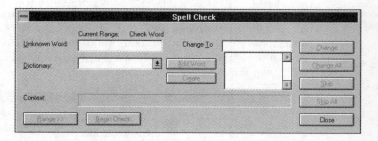

To check selected text, click on the range button and then on Begin Check. When an unknown word is encountered (a word not included in the CorelDRAW! dictionary), the program will make suggestions in the Change To box. If the correct version of the word is shown here, click on it and then on the Change button. You can add an 'unknown' word to the CorelDRAW! dictionary by activating the Add Word button. If the word is spelled correctly (a proper name for instance), you can leave it as it is and continue the spelling check by clicking on the Skip button.

If you simply wish to check a single word, type the word in the Unknown Word box and then click on Begin Check. If the word is correctly spelled, a small message box appears telling you so; other wise, alternatives are suggested in the Change To box.

The basic CorelDRAW! dictionary is reasonably large, but it can be extended even further. To do this, click on the Create button. If you want to add a new dictionary (containing special entries you have specified previously) to the main dictionary for the check, select the dictionary name from the drop-down Dictionary list.

Thesaurus

If a particular word occurs too often in a text, it is advisable to choose a synonym to break the monotony. Use the Text tool to highlight the word which you wish to replace (drag the cursor across the word) and then choose the *Thesaurus* option from the *Text* menu. If CorelDRAW! does not recognise the word a message box will appear indicating that it has no definitions for it.

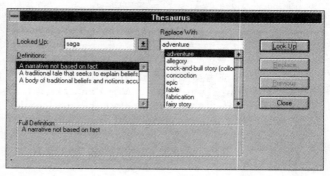

The Definitions box gives a definition of the word in question. This word may have several definitions according to the context. When you click on the appropriate definition, the list of words in the Replace With list will change to conform to the specified definition.

When you click on a word in the Replace With list, it immediately appears in the corresponding text box. Double clicking on a word in this list will provide a list of synonyms for that word, so that you can go 'deeper' in one direction. You can, of course, type another word of your choice in this box, independently of the list.

Clicking on the Replace button will adopt the word into the text.

Find

If you wish to search for a particular word in a text, you can make use of the *Find* function. Place the text cursor in the first word at the beginning of the text, open the *Text* menu and select *Find*. Placing a cross in the Match Case check box will ensure that the search action will take capitals and small letters into account. Click on the Find Next button to start the search. Found text will be selected. Click on Find Next if you want to repeat the search further in the text.

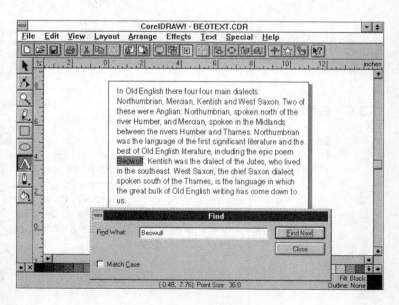

Replace

If you also wish to replace that word with another word, you should choose the *Replace* option. Place the text cursor in the first word of the text, open the *Text* menu and select *Replace*. Specify both the word to be sought and the word which is to replace it. Click on the Find Next button and when the word is found you can click on the Replace button if you do actually wish to implement the action.

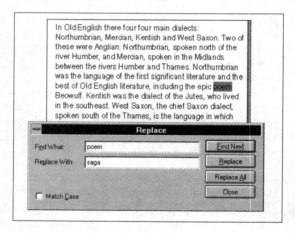

3.8.5 Editing Text

Edit Text

This option (Ctrl+Shift+T shortcut key combination) opens a dialog window in which you can edit the contents and the attributes of the selected artistic or paragraph text. Any modifications here apply to all characters or the entire paragraph. If you wish to alter individual characters, you should select the *Character* option from the *Text* menu or the *Text* roll-up menu.

3.9   The Special Menu

The *Special* menu contains four sections which provide diverse facilities for working with CorelDRAW!.

Preferences

This option opens a dialog window enabling you to specify settings for the display of objects on the screen, and for the execution of certain procedures. This dialog window contains five tabsheets; clicking on the tab at the top will activate the corresponding sheet. The various settings available in this dialog window were discussed in section 2.1.4.

Symbols Roll-Up

If you activate this option, the *Symbols* roll-up menu will appear, providing a large number of symbols which can be inserted into your work.

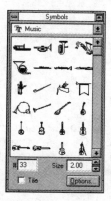

We discussed this function in detail in section 2.3.5.

Presets Roll-Up

You can store certain recurring actions, such as applying colours and shapes, in a *macro* to automise your work. In that case, these actions are implemented with a single mouse click. Select this option (Alt+F5 is the shortcut key combination) to open the roll-up menu. You can then apply the recorded effects, such as fountain fills, to a selected object. In addition, you can also record procedures such as moving, stretching and filling. The standard CorelDRAW! macros can be used as the basis for your own personal macros; adjust them to suit your own requirements.

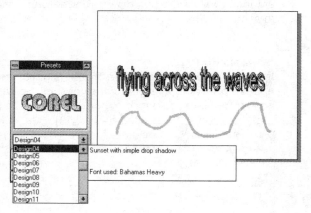

The drop-down list in the roll-up menu contains more than a hundred standard effects. Click on the arrow next to the list to open it and press the cursor keys to browse down through the various options. Some options provide a brief description, which you can also edit by means of the Edit button. Clicking on Apply will apply the effect to the graphic or text object you have selected.

If you wish to create a macro yourself, select the object first. Then click on the Start Recording button and make the modifications you wish to save in the macro. If you use a function which cannot be saved as a macro in CorelDRAW! (such as PowerClips), a window appears to tell you so. When you have carried out all the necessary actions, click on the Stop Recording button which has now replaced Start Recording. Finally, give the macro a name and type any notes you wish to store along with the macro. Click on OK to include the macro in the drop-down list.

Create Pattern, Create Arrow and Create Symbol

The options in the third section of the *Special* menu enable you to create your own patterns, arrows and symbols. We discussed creating patterns in detail in section 2.7.3.

When creating arrows and symbols, create the object you wish to save as an arrow or symbol. Select the object if necessary and select the relevant option from the *Special* menu. If you create an arrow, you will have to confirm this in the subsequent dialog box. You may have to combine the various components into a single object (*Arrange* menu, *Combine* command). An arrow can be edited later in the Outline pen dialog box. If you create a symbol, it will be adopted into the category of your choice and can be used as often as you wish.

Extract

This option enables you to save text objects in the currently active drawing as ASCII text. In that case, you can edit the text further using a word processor.

Merge Back

This option will reverse the process described above. Text which has been modified can be placed back in the drawing.

3.10 The Help Menu

The *Help* menu will produce help and instructions on the screen should you run into difficulties or require additional information.

Contents

Activating this option (shortcut key F1) produces a help window in which the various categories of the Corel-DRAW! Help function are displayed.

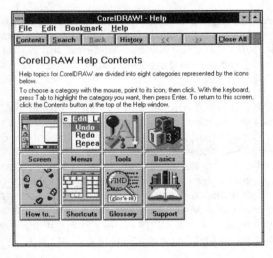

Click on one of the icons to switch to the corresponding help category. The subsequent Overview window contains all the available topics in that category. Switch to a topic by clicking on the relevant title. Procedures and descriptions are shown in the activated window.

Screen/Menu Help

Select this option (shortcut key Shift+F1) to switch immediately to the Help topic which refers to a certain element of the CorelDRAW! interface (symbols, buttons, menu commands etc.) When you select this option the mouse pointer changes into a white arrow with a black question mark, just like the button at the extreme right-hand side of the Ribbon bar. Place the mouse pointer at the screen element about which you want to gain more information, the Ribbon bar for instance, and click. The Help window containing the relevant information appears.

Search For Help On

This option (shortcut key Ctrl+F1) activates an extensive list of terms. Type the topic about which you wish to obtain information in the upper text box. Words which correspond to this entry appear in the alphabetical drop-down list. Select the term you require and click on the Show Topics button. The related topics appear in the lower section of the window.

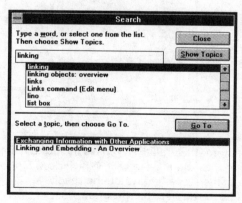

Activate the required topic and click on Go To.

Tutorial

This option activates a tutorial which is directed at users who wish to learn more about working with the program. This option is only available if the Tutorial has actually been installed.

About CorelDRAW!

Activating this option produces a window which gives information about the CorelDRAW! version and the registration data. The System Info button opens a window which gives a complete overview of your computer system.

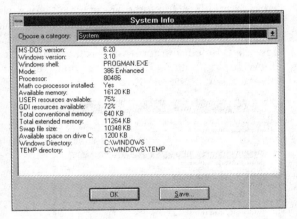

The creators of CorelDRAW! have included a small visual joke in the About CorelDRAW! window. Double click on one of the icons and watch the result.
Press Esc to return to the program.

All programs in the Corel package have a similar *Help* menu.

4 CorelDRAW! - Creating and editing images

In this chapter, we shall use several examples to describe how to create attractive pictures. You can create these pictures on your own computer, step by step; you can also simply load them from the diskette which is available along with this book. You will see that Corel-DRAW! is a professional instrument, ideal for creating, for instance, menu cards, visiting cards or invitations.

Summary of topics dealt with in this chapter:

- creating note paper
- creating a calendar
- creating an advertisement.

4.1 Creating notepaper

We shall begin with a simple example, creating notepaper. Only two basic functions are really important here: selecting a design and positioning the name. The result is shown in the figure below:

Proceed as follows:

1) Start up CorelDRAW! if necessary.
2) Open the *File* menu and select *Mosaic Roll-Up*.
3) Click on the Browse button (the open folder icon in the upper right-hand corner.

4)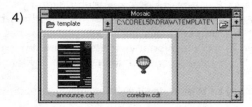

The *Open Collection* dialog window appears. Activate the directory containing the pictures and symbols, [drive]:\CORELDRW\DRAW\CLIPART. If you have a CD ROM, select that drive (in many cases this will be referred to as D:). Insert the first CD and select the \CLIPART directory by double clicking on it. A complete overview of all the available images is given in the ClipArt manual supplied along with CorelDRAW!. Make sure that All Files is shown in the List Files of Type section and select an appropriate category. The screen will look something like this:

5) Click on OK. The images from the selected category are then displayed in the *Mosaic* window. If you
wish, you can enlarge the window to show more images simultaneously. Select a drawing and drag it
using the left mouse button to the drawing window.

6) The drawing is now displayed in the CorelDRAW!
working area. Activate the text tool to type a name
and an address of your choice on the notepaper;
click at the desired position.

7) If you wish to edit the text, open the *Edit* menu and
select *Character*.

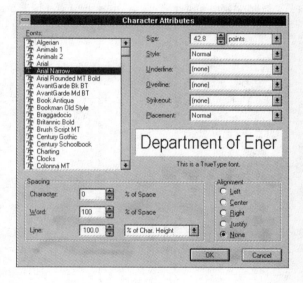

8) In our example, we have chosen the Arial Narrow
font. You can, of course, select any font which you
find attractive. Click on OK to apply it.

9) Now you only need to save the drawing. Open the
File menu and select *Save As*. In the *Print* dialog
window, you can determine how many copies of the
notepaper are to be printed.

There are approximately 22,000 ClipArt images which you can use to make pictures. We shall also make use of these in the next example.

4.2 Creating a calendar

The figure below shows the picture for the month of September in a 1995 calendar based on famous statements. We have again made use of the ClipArt images supplied along with CorelDRAW!. It is also possible to work with self-made drawings or with photographs (with PHOTO-PAINT) instead.

Proceed as follows. To create the calendar, you need various guidelines to position the days of the week and the numbers.

1) First create a grid with guidelines. Open the *Layout* menu and specify the guideline positions, both for the horizontal and the vertical guidelines. Type the

position and click on the Add button. The line is
added to the list.

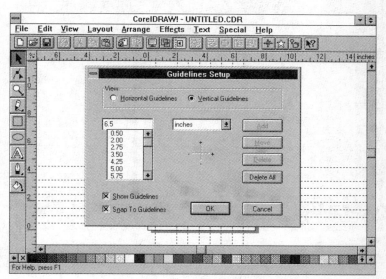

You can also do this by dragging the guidelines one by
one from the Rulers along the top and flanking the left-
hand side of the window. (If the Rulers are not displayed,
open the *View* menu and click on *Rulers*. The guidelines
should be positioned as shown in the top figure overleaf.

2) For your own reference, you can specify the grid or-
    igin at the upper intersection of the guidelines by
    clicking at the intersection point of the two Rulers
    and dragging the two lines to cover the guidelines
    you placed.

3) Now define the attributes for the font and the font
    size. Click on the Text tool, open the *Text* menu and
    select *Character*. The *Character Attributes* window
    appears.

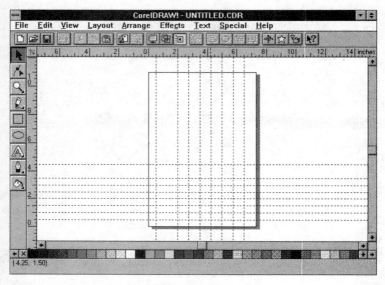

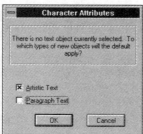

4) Confirm this by clicking on OK. Now select Brush Script from the font list and specify font size 40. Click on OK.

5) Click on the Text Tool if necessary and place the cursor at the required position on the uppermost guideline. Type the month. Click on the Zoom Tool to get a better view of the document if necessary.

6) Move to the lower lines to type the days there. Double click on the Text Tool to open the *Text* roll-up

menu. Decrease the font size to 24 points. Type the days, clicking on the appropriate position each time. You can do this reasonably approximately because the text will be attracted to the guidelines automatically (*Snap To Guidelines* option, *Layout* menu).

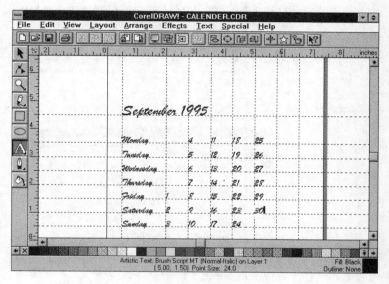

You have now made a structure for one month. Save it under the name SEP95.CDR. You can use this structure to create the other months.

7) If you now wish to create a page for October, you will have to move the numbers downwards since the first of October will begin on a Sunday. Drag a marquee frame across the numbers (first click on the Pick Tool) and press the Del key. Also delete 'September 1995'. Enter the relevant data in the existing structure.

8) The guidelines have done their work and can now retire gracefully. You can activate the Pick Tool and drag them one by one back to the Ruler. However, this is a bit laborious. It is easier to make use of the different layers. Open the *Layout* menu and select *Layers Roll-Up*. Double click on Guides and deactivate the Visible option in the *Edit Layers* dialog box.

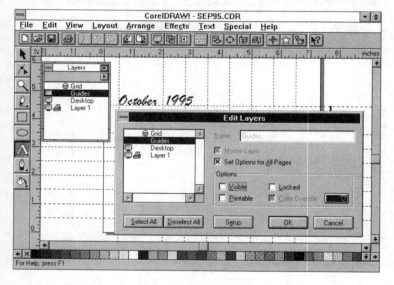

9) Close the window by clicking on OK. The guidelines disappear. But you can easily make them visible again by reversing this action. This is done by opening the *Layout* menu, selecting *Layers Roll-Up*, double clicking on Guides and activating the Visible box again. Click on Layer 1 to continue working on this layer.

10) Now you should import a picture for your calendar. This will be placed above your actual calendar. Select a picture from the ClipArt directory, either via *File, Import* or *Mosaic Roll-Up*.

When you have imported the picture, place it at the required position. You can also apply effects or add text. Save it once you are satisfied. It can then be printed.

4.3 Creating an advert

Creating a drawing for an advert is not an easy job. This type of drawing should exert a certain amount of influence, presenting the product in such a way that an impression lingers with the public. Adverts should encourage people to purchase products or to present people or instances in a positive manner. We shall describe a text for environmental protection.

Regardless of the actual theme, an advert must have a certain basis. Images and text must be clearly visible. The figure below displays the basic elements schematically.

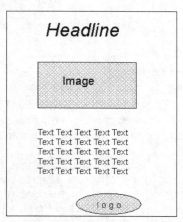

If you examine advertisements in magazines, you will see that these four elements occur in almost every one. The main slogan of the advert should be reproduced at the position of the *headline*. The image should correlate to the headline and express it in one way or another. The text underneath should provide additional information. Details are given or the slogan is explained. The logo should be present to provide a cumulative recognition factor.

We shall describe an advertisement based on this scheme.

1) We shall first create a headline. Select the Text Tool and place the cursor at the top left-hand corner of the page. Type the text. Press Enter to move on to the next line.

2) Click on the Pick Tool and select the text. Double click on the Text Tool to open the *Text* roll-up menu. Select a font which is suitable to the contents of the text. In our case, we have selected Footlight to emphasise an everyday situation. Click on Apply. If the text does not fit onto the line, you can always reduce the point size or even change the font quite easily. We can always return to this element when looking

for a balanced whole when the rest of the advert has been created.

3) Now open the ClipArt directory containing images (use *Import* or *Mosaic Roll-Up* from the *File* menu). We have chosen Maid from the \CLIPART\PEO-PLE\WORKERS directory since it fits in nicely with the text. Photographs are also supplied on CD along with the CorelDRAW! package. These are normally edited using CorelPHOTO-PAINT, but they can also be loaded in CorelDRAW!.

4) If you wish to load a photograph, use the *Import* command from the *File* menu. You will have to define the TIF extension for pixel-based images or PCX for photographs from PHOTO-PAINT in the List Files of Type box.

5) Click on OK to import a picture once you have found a suitable one or drag it into the drawing window from the *Mosaic* roll-up window. You do not need to precisely define the image size as yet.

6) Now type the supporting text. Click on the Text Tool and activate the Paragraph Text Tool. Use the mouse to draw the required frame. When you release the mouse button, a flashing text cursor is displayed in the upper left-hand corner, ready to begin on the first line. Type the text you want.

7) Now the three different components have to be correctly placed. Click on the objects and drag them to the required positions. Use the handles to enlarge and reduce them.

8) To slant the text, you have to apply a small trick. Select the Rectangle Tool and drag a close-fitting frame around the text. Click on the colour white in the colour palette. The text is now covered by the white frame. Select the frame, open the *Arrange* menu, select *Order* and click on *To Back* in the subsequent submenu.

9) Select both text and rectangle (hold down the Shift key and watch the status line), open the *Arrange*

menu and select *Group*. The two objects now form one group. Move it a little to the left.

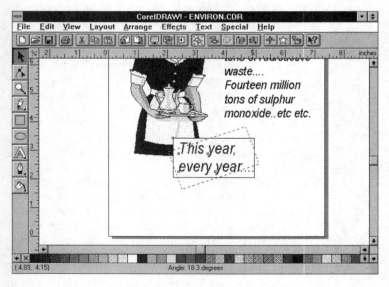

10) If you now click on the grouped objects again, the small black blocks change into the rotation and skew arrows. Click on the arrow at the right-hand side and drag it upwards.

11) Due to the fact that the text is now grouped with the frame, it has gained a white background, even on top of the other figure. This makes it clearly legible.

12) Finally, create a logo and place it in the lower right-hand corner of the advertisement.

Experiment with the various elements of the drawing until you are satisfied with the result.

5 CorelCHART - Creating charts

CorelCHART is a powerful instrument for making charts and diagrams for the office or the company. The large number of diagrams available and the ease of operation put CorelCHART at the same level as other professional chart-oriented programs.

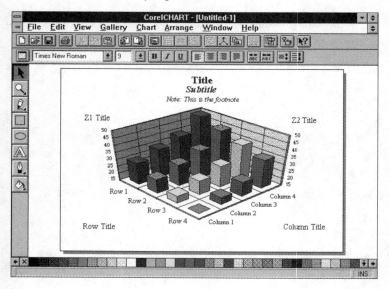

Using CorelCHART, you can make all kinds of charts and diagrams, including bar and pie charts, line and scatter charts in two- and three-dimensional forms and bar, and many more. We shall discuss the possibilities in this chapter.

The topics in this chapter:
- the basic chart elements
- creating a chart

- saving and printing charts
- types of charts
- drawing tools

Actually constructing a chart is extremely simple and straightforward. Open the *File* menu and select *New*. Select the required type of chart from the Gallery list. Each category has a number of variations. These are shown in the right-hand section under Chart Types.

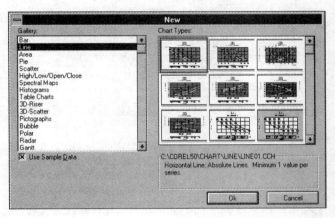

It is possible to open a chart either with or without data. Opening a chart with data has the advantage that later you only need to type over the data.

Entering or altering data takes place in a worksheet that resembles a spreadsheet in a spreadsheet program. You can not only enter data, you can also make calculations.

Once a chart has been created, it can easily be formatted further. All familiar types of diagrams and charts, such as bar and pie charts, line diagrams etc. are available in two- and three-dimensional display. When you select a

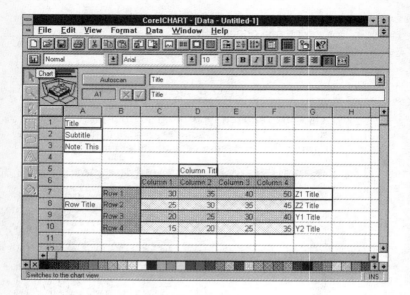

new chart type for your data, the information is analysed and a new chart is created to present these data as accurately as possible.

In addition, you can create and edit free graphic objects and texts by mean of the tools in the toolbox. A great advantage of CorelCHART is that you can use the *Copy Chart* command from the *Edit* menu to copy an entire chart to the Windows Clipboard. You can then, for instance, copy it to CorelDRAW! using the *Paste Special* option from the *Edit* menu in that program. This kind of link makes it possible for any changes to the data in the original chart to be automatically passed on to the chart in CorelDRAW!.

This indicates how versatile CorelCHART is. We shall briefly describe several new concepts and aspects of charts. Subsequently, we shall describe the various commands available in the light of practical examples.

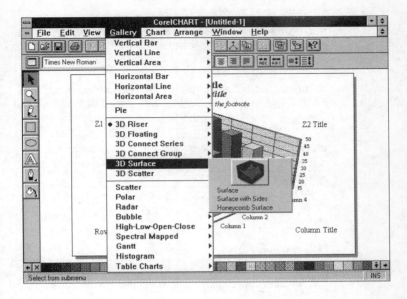

5.1 The basic elements of charts and diagrams

When constructing charts and diagrams, certain elements recur. The following figure gives an indication of these types of elements.

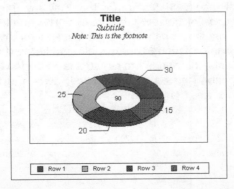

Thus, in each chart or diagram, there is a title, subtitle and a footnote, although these can differ according to each diagram.

The charts and diagrams that can be created in Corel-CHART, partly in combination with CorelDRAW!, can be roughly subdivided into the following groups:

diagrams	text charts	cartograms
bar charts	table charts	spectral maps
line diagrams	free text	maps
circle and pie charts		
area charts		
scatter charts		
high/low/open/ close charts		
histograms		
3D riser charts		
3D scatter charts		

5.1.1 Diagrams

Diagrams can be roughly subdivided into axis and pie charts. These have in common that they are graphic representations of certain table values. The numerical values are visually translated into areas, lines or points and mutual comparison indicates their significance. With axis diagrams, the values are set against the different axes. A distinction can be made between two- and three-dimensional axis diagrams:

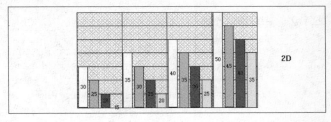

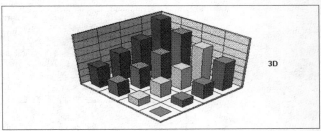

A spatial effect can be realised with bar charts by means of the '3D-Riser'.
CorelCHART can also reproduce a 'real' 3D display of points and areas in space.

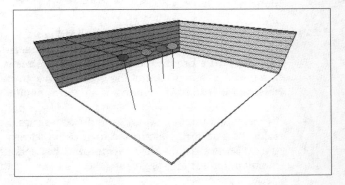

5.1.2 Pie charts

In the case of pie charts, the most important feature is the totality of the data. The figure below illustrates this:

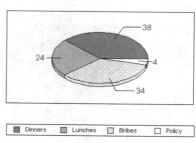

Here too, you find a title, subtitle and footnote. In addition, the various segments give an indication of their significance, often text along with percentages. It is also possible to accentuate individual segments by lifting them out of the pie.

It is often necessary to allocate more than one piece of data to points in pie charts and axis diagrams. Additional series can be created for this. The figure below shows the caviar consumption of the Clarke family over the last few years. Three categories are shown in each unit.

In cases like these, it is often not possible to place the relevant categories along the axes. Accordingly, the explanation is positioned elsewhere so that the chart remains uncluttered. This explanation is referred to as the 'legend'.

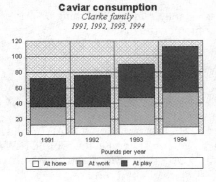

5.1.3 Text charts

We shall not deal with text charts here. Free texts and charts have few common features, and moreover, we dealt with this type of presentation in the section concerning CorelDRAW!.

5.1.4 Spectral maps and cartograms

Spectral maps can only be shown as tables in Corel-CHART. In this, certain colour values are assigned to the cells in a table. These colours represent fixed values. An example of this could be the number of visitors to a particular section of an exhibition over a certain period of time. Dark patches represent many visitors and light ones stand for less intensive interest.

You cannot create cartograms in CorelCHART, although you can do so in CorelDRAW!. Select the required map from the symbol library containing the maps. You will then have to carry out the calculations yourself which the computer would normally perform. You can display the frequencies of certain characteristic features of each region on the map. Place the frequencies under one another and assign colours or grey tints to them. Subsequently, allocate the same colour to the corresponding region on the map.

5.2 Creating a chart

To create a chart, proceed as follows:

1) Start up the CorelCHART program by double clicking on its icon in the CorelDRAW! group.

2) Open the *File* menu in which you can select the type of chart required.

3) Ensure that a cross is placed in the Use Sample Data check box so that the chart can be opened with a standard structure. You can alter the data later; otherwise only an empty worksheet will appear so that you will have to structure the chart yourself right from the beginning.

4) For this example, click on Bar in the Gallery section and activate the first type in the upper left-hand corner. Click on OK. (See the upper figure on the opposite page.)

A bar chart appears based on standard data and chart elements. We shall alter these by typing over the data.

5) Click on the small table icon above the Pick Tool arrow in the upper left-hand corner of the screen. A worksheet appears.

The worksheet resembles a Microsoft Excel worksheet. It contains rows (indicated by numbers) and columns (indicated by letters), producing a grid on the screen. The points of intersection are called 'cells'. Thus, each cell has its own address, consisting of a combination of the column and row references, for example A1 or G7.

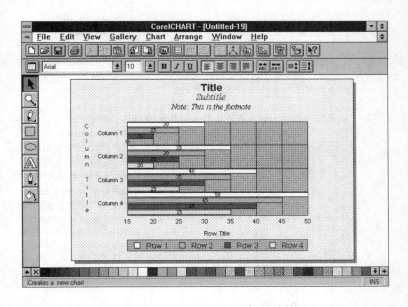

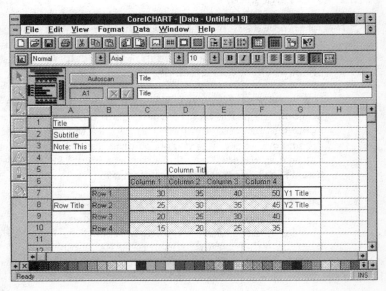

All the data which are to be used for the chart are entered in these cells. It is also possible to adopt data from other applications. Each cell can contain a character or a value for the chart. Prior to entering data in a cell, you have to activate that cell first.

6) Click on cell A1. The value or text in the cell is reproduced on the bar just above the worksheet. In this case, cell A1 contains the title of the chart; it is a new chart so only 'Title' is shown here. In the schematic representation of the chart, next to the Pick Tool, the currently active row is marked in red.

7) To assign a new title to the chart, simply type the new title over the previous one. The alteration is shown immediately on the input bar.

8) Confirm the input by pressing Enter. The text is then transferred to the cell.

5.2.1   The worksheet

All standard sample charts have the same construction. Cell A1 contains the title, cell A2 the subtitle. If you had opened a chart without using the sample data, the worksheet would have been empty.

It is not necessary to type the data at exactly the same positions as in the sample chart. Each cell in the worksheet can be freely defined. You can, for instance, type the title in cell B17 if you wish. Prior to describing the exact layout, we shall conclude this example, which illustrates the viewing habits of four families.

9) Type the following text in the appropriate cells:
Title (cell A1):   Television addiction
Subtitle (cell A2):   hours per week
Footnote (cell A3): Source: TV Research
Row Title (cell A8):   HOURS

Adopt the data shown in the figure below, and delete the Column Title:

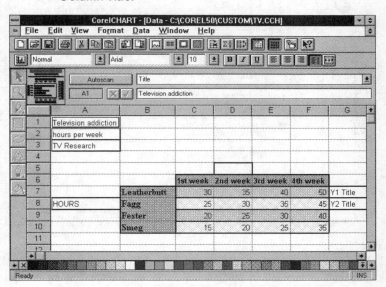

We have widened the A and B columns to present the data more clearly. (Place the mouse pointer on the line between the column letters and drag it to the right.)

10) When your worksheet resembles the example, click on the chart icon in the upper left-hand corner of the window. CorelCHART switches over to the chart mode.

All elements are situated at the defined positions. But the chart is not very clear. The bars could be thicker, the X axis, showing the number of hours, should range from 0 to 50 (instead of 15 to 50) so that the viewing time in the first week of the family Smeg is also shown, and the legend is not very legible.

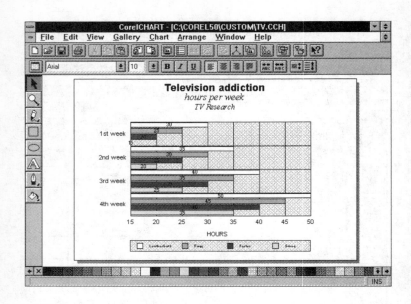

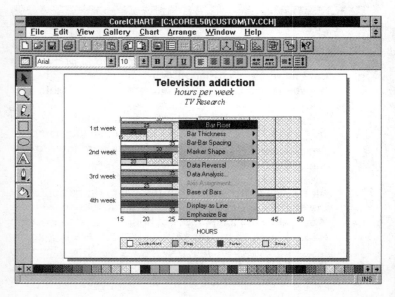

To make these alterations, press the right mouse button
to open the context-oriented formatting function. Move
the mouse pointer to the position where you wish to
make the alterations and click on the right mouse button.
An editing menu appears, providing options which are
applicable to that position.

Click on the required option in the menu. In our case, we
wish to alter the bar thickness.

1) Place the mouse pointer on any bar and click on the
   right mouse button.
2) Select the *Bar Thickness* and click on *Maximum* in
   the submenu.
3) Now click on the right mouse button anywhere within the diagram but not on a bar.

4) Select the *Display Status* option. We wish to remove the numbers from the bars to give the chart a
   less cluttered appearance. Remove the cross in the
   Display box under Data Values.

You can also activate and deactivate all the other components of a chart by clicking on the corresponding check
boxes. Make other changes if you wish, and then click on
OK.

To change the scale of a value axis, click with the right
mouse button on one of the values along the X axis and
select the *Scale Range* option from the submenu. The
dialog window of the same name appears. Click on Manual Scale and specify 0 as the minimum value:

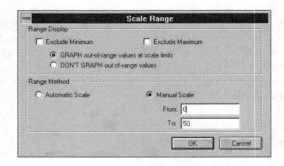

Click on OK. The chart will now look something like this:

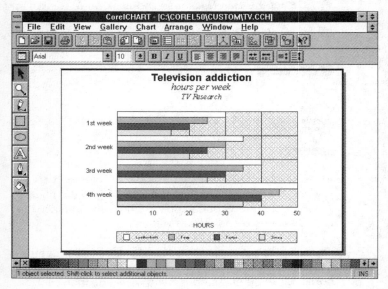

Finally, click on the legend using the right mouse button. Select *Legend* from the menu and deactivate the Autofit Legend Text option. Then activate the Text Below Marker option and click on OK. Now you will be able to adjust the size of the font by means of the Font Size drop-down list on the Formatting toolbar. First click on one of the names to activate it and then select size 10 from the list. The final version of the chart will look like this:

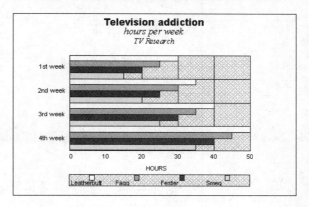

You can use this procedure to create and edit other types of chart. We shall now describe another method, that of creating a chart without making use of sample data. The chart will eventually look like this:

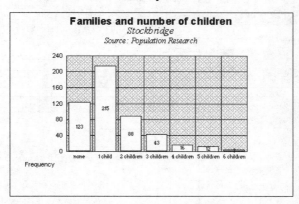

The chart is based on the following data:

Number of children	Frequency
0	123
1	215
2	88
3	43
4	16
5	12
6 and more	3

The first steps are identical to those in the previous example. Start up the program if necessary and open the *File* menu. Select *New*.

3) This time ensure that the Use Sample Data check box is deactivated.

4) Click on Bar in the Gallery list. Double click on the chart in the middle of the second row. An empty worksheet appears.

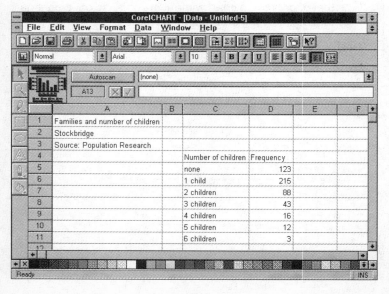

5) Type the following data:

6) Click on the Autoscan button. This instructs Corel-CHART to look for the separate components of the chart, such as title and subtitle and to define the cells used for these.

7) Click on the Chart icon in the upper left-hand part

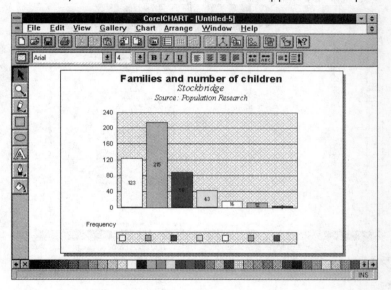

of the screen. The following chart appears:
We shall make a few changes to this basic figure.

8) Switch back to the worksheet. Open the *Data* menu and select *Data Orientation*.

9) Activate the Columns are Series option button in the subsequent dialog window and confirm this by clicking on OK. Then switch back to the chart.

10) In this case, the legend serves no purpose. Remove it by clicking on it with the right mouse button and deactivating the Display Legend option.

11) If the word 'Frequency' is displayed in the middle of the chart, click on it to activate it and drag it to the

proper place under the Y axis.

12) Adjust the size of the text under the bars by clicking on one of them and then on the Font Size drop-down list. Select size 8. All the text is immediately

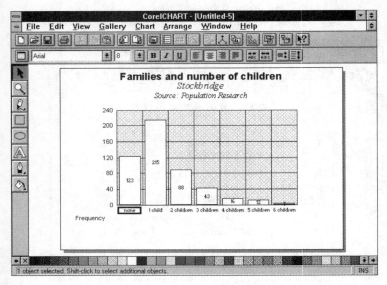

adjusted.

The Autoscan function alleviates the work when you are creating a chart, but this function is only really convenient when a title, subtitle, footnote and data have to be allocated. Certain conditions have to be fulfilled in this procedure. The title, subtitle and footnote have to be typed directly under one another. The table containing the data must also form an entity, so that CorelCHART can recognise the table by means of the column and row headings and the numeric values. If you wish to enter additional text, you have to define this separately in the worksheet.

We shall extend the chart by adding titles for the Y axis.

Switch to the worksheet and pay particular attention to the upper section displaying the schematic diagram and the other data to the right of this.

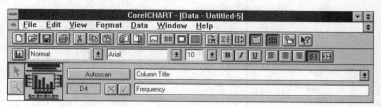

Select the cell D4, Frequency. Click on the arrow pointing downwards to the right of the text box containing the words 'Column Title'. A list of all available graphic elements appears. Select Y1 Title. This action defines the word 'Frequency' as being the Y axis title. The small schematic diagram indicates, in red, where this title will be displayed. In this way, you can position each component in the chart and change its appearance (font, font size etc.) later in the chart mode.

5.2.2 Saving and printing a chart

While working, you should save your chart regularly, so that you will not lose too much if the computer freezes or a power failure occurs.
Proceed as follows to save the chart (from the worksheet or the chart window):

1) Open the *File* menu and select *Save As*.
2) Specify the drive and the directory where the file is to be stored.
3) Type the file name (maximum eight characters).

We have saved the chart under the name CHILDREN. If you wish, you can enter a brief description of the file in

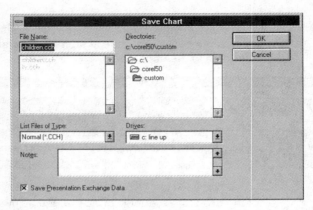

the Notes section at the bottom of the dialog window.

Printing a file is just as easy as saving it. First switch to the window containing the data you want to print (either the worksheet or the chart). Open the *File* menu and select *Print*. The *Print* dialog window appears, in which you can specify a number of options. The most important options have already been made in the Windows Control Panel. You only need to make adjustments for the current chart. For example, you can make a trial printout with a low print quality of 75 dpi. Click on OK when the settings are suited to the chart.

5.3 Selecting a different type of chart

You can easily convert an existing chart to another type of chart. Since the data have already been recorded, the program only needs to make calculations to place the display elements at the appropriate positions. Sometimes adjustments have to be made later because overlaps may occur when axis titles and legends are moved. We shall continue with our example. Open the chart from the previous exercise if it is not currently active.

1) Open the *Gallery* menu.
2) A list of available types of chart is presented. Click on the *3D Riser* option.

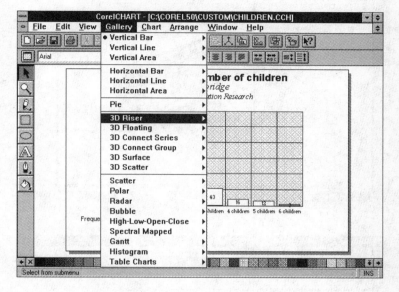

3) Click on *Bars*, holding down the mouse button. A small sample chart is shown above the submenu to give you an indication of how the chart will appear. If you move down through the submenu using the cursor, the other sample charts are displayed.
4) When you release the mouse button, the existing diagram is replaced by the chosen type. The existing data are used in the recalculation. The result in this particular case is shown overleaf.

If this display is not exactly what you want, you can use the *Chart* menu to choose a different perspective. Click on *Preset Viewing Angles*. Here too, you can see a preview of the style by moving through the list by pressing the cursor keys (see the lower figure overleaf).

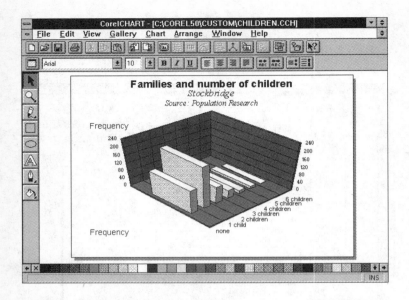

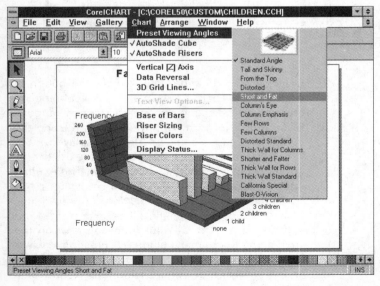

5.4   Changing perspective

When you are working with 3D charts, you can select a predefined perspective. However, you can also modify the viewing angle size and position to meet your own requirements. To do so, open the *View* menu and select *3D Roll-Up*. The following roll-up menu then appears on the screen:

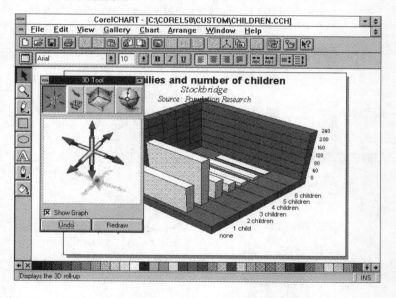

This 3D tool has four functions. Click on the first button at the top left-hand corner (if this button is not already active). This function enables you to move a three-dimensional chart in various directions. Click on one of the red arrows to do this. A placement frame appears in the chart indicating where the chart will be positioned when you release the mouse button. When the chart has reached the required position, click on the Redraw button in the *3D Tool* roll-up menu. The chart is then redrawn.

You can restore the original position of the chart by clicking on the Undo button prior to redrawing the screen. The Show Graph option enables you to view the chart while you are altering it, or restrict the display to the placement frame only. The chart is always fully redrawn when you click on one of the buttons.

The second button along the top enables you to change the position, perspective and size of the chart. These options overlap those produced by the first option to a certain extent.

Here too, you click on the red arrows to make alterations to the chart. The functions correspond to those described above.

The third button enables you to change the cubic proportions of the chart.

The 3D axes and the base of the figure are changed by clicking on the arrows.

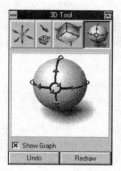

The fourth button enables you to rotate the chart.

5.5   CorelCHART toolbox

We became acquainted with the toolbox when working with CorelDRAW!. CorelCHART also provides the same kinds of tools, corresponding to a large degree with those in CorelDRAW!. Accordingly, we shall confine ourselves here to an outline of the differences. The Pick, the Ellipse and the Rectangle Tools are identical to those in CorelDRAW!. (See section 2.3.1 for a detailed description of the tools.)

5.5.1   The Zoom Tool

You can enlarge or reduce the entire display of the chart by clicking on the Zoom Tool. A flyout menu appears when you click on the tool.

Click on the icon with the plus sign and then on the chart if you wish to enlarge the display. Click on the icon with the minus sign to reduce the display (again). The

1:1 button shows the chart in real size and the button with the page icon, the Zoom to Page Tool, brings all objects into view.

5.5.2 The Pencil Tool

When you click on the Pencil Tool and hold down the mouse button, a flyout menu appears, containing three options.

To draw a freehand line, a straight line or an arrow, click on the first (freehand) or second icon (straight line). Move the mouse pointer to the chart and click to determine the starting position. Drag the mouse pointer to the new position to draw the line.

If you wish to draw a polygon (several-sided figure), click on the third icon. Place the mouse pointer at the required starting position and click. Move the mouse pointer to the end point of the first side and click again. Continue this process until only the last side has to be drawn. Double click on the mouse button and the program draws the last line automatically between that position and the starting point.

5.5.3 The Text Tool

You can enter text in a chart or alter existing text by means of the Text Tool. Click on the Text Tool (the letter A) and move the mouse pointer to the required position.

Typing new text

The cursor has the shape of a cross at first. Move it to the starting point. Click, hold down the mouse button and drag a frame in which the text is to be placed.. When you release the mouse button, a flashing text cursor is shown at the starting position, ready for input. The size of the text is automatically adjusted to fit the frame. Conclude the text input by clicking on the Pick Tool.

Altering existing text

Place the cursor on the existing text, on the title or subtitle of a chart for instance. Click at the position where you wish to make changes. The existing text is selected although you cannot see this. The text to be inserted will be assigned the format of the existing text. You can press Del or Backspace to delete characters. You enter other characters by simply typing them. Conclude the input by clicking on the Pick Tool.

Changing the text format

There are a number of options available in CorelCHART for changing the format of existing text. These are shown on the Formatting bar.

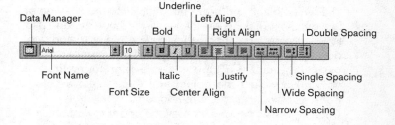

Prior to altering the text format, you first have to select the text in question by means of the Pick Tool. The text is then enclosed by eight handles. Click on the required button on the Formatting toolbar. The changes are automatically applied to the selected text. If you wish to undo the changes, click on the same button immediately or select *Undo* from the *Edit* menu.

In this way, you can change the font and the font size, and also the colour of the text by selecting a new colour from the colour palette.

5.5.4   The Outline Tool

The Outline Tool is primarily used to define the thickness of a line or arrow. When you click on the Outline Tool, the following flyout menu appears:

The facilities provided here largely correspond to those in CorelDRAW!. The X with the square will define the outline of the selected object as being zero. The icons with the increasingly thicker lines apply the corresponding line thickness to the selected object.

The white, black and grey tints determine the shading of the outline. Clicking on the Outline Color button (2nd row, extreme left) opens the *Outline Color* dialog window where you can allocate any of a large number of colours to the outline. There is also a shortcut method of doing this: select the object and then select a colour from the colour palette at the bottom of the screen.
Clicking on the second icon on the upper row opens the *Pen* roll-up menu. See section 2.6 for more information about this roll-up menu.

5.5.5   The Fill Tool

The Fill Tool enables you to fill a selected object with shading or colour, or to assign no filling at all. When you click on the Fill Tool, a flyout menu appears, also almost identical to that in CorelDRAW!.

Clicking on the first icon, the Solid Fill button, opens the *Uniform Fill* dialog window from which you can make a choice out of a whole range of colours.

The No Fill button (with the X) removes the filling in the selected object. You can also select the vector-based filling (with the diagonal double-headed arrow), bitmap effects (chess board), fountain fills or texture fills. Clicking on the Fill Roll-Up button opens a roll-up menu in which all these facilities are available.

You can place this roll-up menu at any position on the screen, or roll it up when it is not in use. This is done by clicking on the small arrow pointing upwards in the upper right-hand corner. The menu is constructed as a multi-functional building block. We shall demonstrate this in the light of a practical example.

1) First draw a rectangle on the screen using the Rectangle Tool.
2) Select this rectangle using the Pick Tool.
3) Open the roll-up menu.

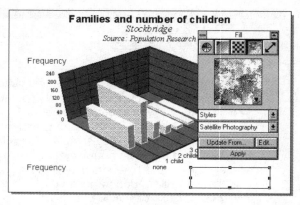

4) Click on the Fountain Fill button in the roll-up menu, the second button from the left. A pattern appears in the preview window. Other patterns are displayed on buttons which are shown in the lower section of the roll-up menu.

5) Select a fountain fill and specify the colours which determine the overflow.

6) Click on the Apply button to fill the rectangle with the chosen pattern. You can also click on the Edit button to modify the filling to suit your own requirements.

Applying ClipArt is also very easy. In the example shown opposite, we selected a section of a pie chart (having opened a new file) using the Pick Tool. Then we opened the Fill Tool flyout menu and clicked on the Pictograph Roll-Up button (upper row, extreme right).

We selected a pictograph by clicking on the small arrow in the lower right-hand corner of the image and choosing a suitable one from the list. Clicking on the Apply button placed it in the chart. When the chart is enlarged by means of the Zoom Tool, it will look like the lower figure on the opposite page.

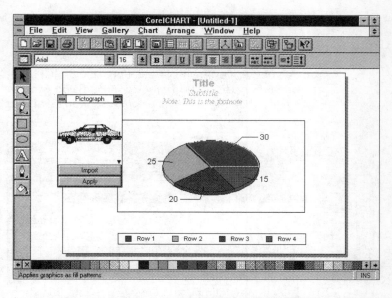

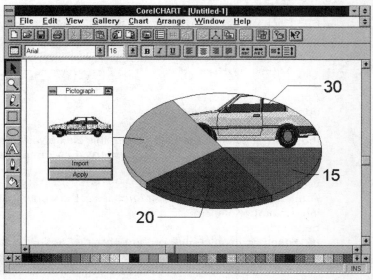

5.5.6 Calculations in CorelCHART

You can perform extensive calculations in CorelCHART. You can make use of the *Enter Formula* dialog window (via the *Data* menu) to enter extensive formulas and to

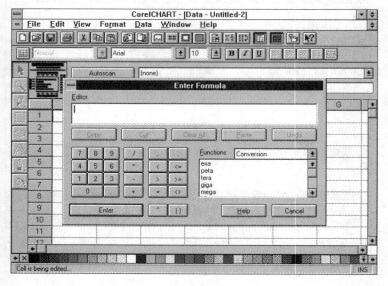

activate special functions.

For more detailed information about this dialog window, see *Help* menu, *Spreadsheet Functions*, *Enter Formula dialog box*.

You can however, simply enter formulas in the worksheet straightaway.

An example: Imagine that you are on a diet and wish to calculate the loss of weight, in percentual terms, in the course of a week. CorelCHART can work this out quickly and flawlessly. We know that the starting weight was 78 kilograms and the final weight was 72 kilos. The formula can be expressed as follows:

percentual loss = (original value - new value)/original val-

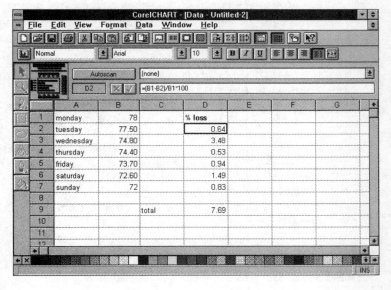

*ue * 100*

The calculation is carried out as follows:

1) Open the *File* menu and select *New*.
2) Ensure that there is no cross in the Use Sample Data check box. Click on OK. An empty worksheet appears.
3) Fill in the data as shown in columns A and B.
4) We shall now calculate the percentual weight loss for each day. Activate cell D2 by clicking on it. Type an equals sign to instruct the program that a formula is going to be entered.

5) Type the formula to conform to the expression shown above. In our example, the formula is shown on the formula bar, =(B1-B2)/B1*100.

6) Press Enter. The calculation is implemented and the cursor moves downwards to the next cell.

7) Move back to cell D2 and click on the Copy button on the Standard toolbar (6th from the left). The formula is copied to the Clipboard.

8) Move down to cell D3 and click on the Paste button on the Standard toolbar (7th from the left). Corel-CHART automatically adjusts the formula to suit the new cell (=(B2-B3)/B2*100).

9) Move down to each new cell and click on the Paste button each time. The appropriate formula is entered in the new cell each time.

10) Enter a new formula in cell D9 for the total loss (Original value minus final value etc.)

Instead of using the Copy and Paste buttons, you can also use the *Copy* and *Paste Data* options from the *Edit* menu.

There are a number of rules you should keep in mind with formulas:

- they must always begin with an equals sign;
- spaces are not allowed in formulas;
- you can edit formulas by pressing F2.

6 CorelPHOTO-PAINT - Editing photographs

The CorelPHOTO-PAINT program provides a kind of electronic darkroom for editing digitally-saved photographs. You can, for instance, retouch or distort photographs. We shall give an example of this shortly.

There are an enormous number of ways of editing photographs. Electronic editing makes it possible to display certain parts of the photograph more sharply or more vaguely, or to invert, mirror, rotate them, edit the contrast and brightness and apply various predefined special effects. In addition, you can also modify a photograph using a pencil, airbrush, brush or spray. Sections of a photograph can be cut out and inserted into other photographs.

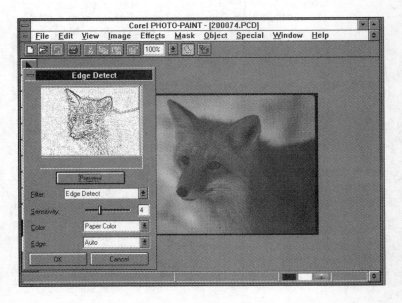

Photographs can not only be edited, they can also be assigned text in combination with CorelDRAW! or Corel-VENTURA. You should first create the text and then import the photographs into the text.

You can also edit and compile photographs in such a way that you can gather them together to form an automatic photography display, running under the Corel-SHOW program (see chapter 7).

And if you wish, you can simply use CorelPHOTO-PAINT as a graphic program. Compared to Windows Paintbrush, CorelPHOTO-PAINT provides more facilities, although it is based on the pixel technique just like Paintbrush. The possibility of editing individual pixels, however, is almost unlimited.

We shall now give a brief example of the possibilities of CorelPHOTO-PAINT.
The football club Everlive FC is suffering from a decline in the number of spectators. Good old-fashioned kick and rush doesn't seem to work anymore in these more sophisticated days and the team is anchored at the foot of the division. The board of directors, unfortunately, is relying on top attendances to pay for the rash of new players this season. An idea is born. An open day is to be organised in conjunction with the supporters club. Folders will be handed out and a slide show will be presented in the form of a quiz.

The local photography shop is able to place normal photographs on a CD, so that they are available in digital form. The club has a CD ROM drive (satisfying the XA standard and suitable for multisession), and is thus able to edit these photographs digitally as described above. It is now not difficult for the board of directors to construct a quiz in which the heads of the players have been placed on the wrong bodies. The participants in the quiz have to place the right heads on the right bodies. The winner receives a free season ticket; the runner-up receives two season tickets.

Topics in this chapter:
- the program interface
- the toolbox
- the colour palette
- functions for editing photographs
- filter functions
- opening, saving and printing images.

6.1   The program interface

Start up CorelPHOTO-PAINT by double clicking on the program icon in the group window. The CorelPHOTO-PAINT working area appears.

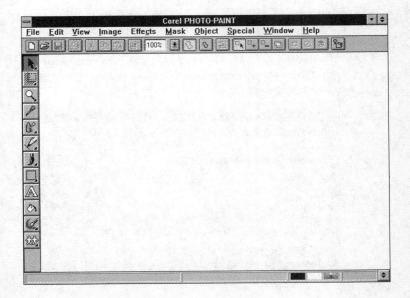

The program interface has, just like the other applications in the CorelDRAW! package, a toolbox, menu bar,
roll-up menus and a drawing window. If you open the *File*
menu and select *New*, a dialog window appears in which
you can make specifications for the new image.

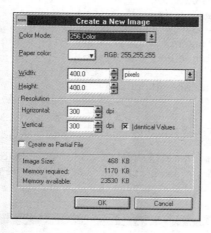

Specify the values for the width, height and resolution of
the new image. Specify the type of display you require in
the Color Mode drop-down list. You can also create images as partial files.

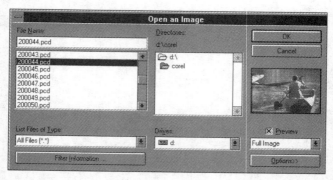

You can open an existing file by opening the *File* menu and selecting *Open*.

Clicking on the Options button extends the dialog window to produce more information about the images available.

In principle, you can open each file as a Full Image, as a Partial Area, a Crop or a Resample. The Partial Area option is very suitable for working with large files since you can work more quickly and then reintegrate the modified area into the complete image once again. With images larger than 16 Mb, the Partial Area option is activated automatically.

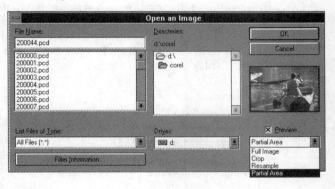

The toolbox
The toolbox contains the tools for working in CorelPHO-TO-PAINT. If a small triangle is also displayed on an icon in the toolbox, a flyout menu will appear when you click on that button and hold the mouse button down for a moment. You can subsequently select the icons in the flyout menu.

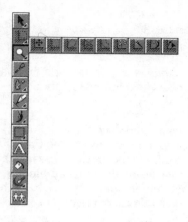

You can leave the toolbox as it is at the left-hand side of the screen, but you can also move it to another position on the screen. To do so, open the *View* menu and select *Toolbox* and then *Floating*. The *Visible* option enables you to display or hide the toolbar.

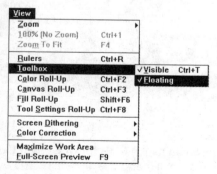

If you choose *Floating* you can drag the toolbox to another position by clicking on the frame. The control menu button in this toolbox enables you to display all the options provided by the toolbox. This is done by clicking on the *Grouped* option in the Control menu.

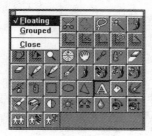

To edit an image, you first have to create one, or open an existing image. We shall demonstrate the most important CorelPHOTO-PAINT functions using a scanned photograph. You can apply the procedure directly on the computer. You may have a scanned photograph you wish to use; we have taken a file from the laser disk supplied along with the CorelDRAW! package.

An existing file is opened by opening the *File* menu and selecting *Open*. Ensure that All Files is displayed in the List Files of Type box. You will then obtain a complete overview of all the available pixel files. Click on a file and then on the Options button. The dialog window is extended with a section showing additional information about the chosen file. Select Full Image if necessary from the drop-down list under the Preview check box.

Click on OK to actually open the file. The *Photo CD Options* dialog window may appear in which you can make further specifications concerning the display of the photograph. Make any changes to these standard settings if you wish and click on OK. A dialog window may *appear* indicating that the image is read-only. Click on OK to acknowledge this. The photograph appears in its own frame in the CorelPHOTO-PAINT window in its original size unless otherwise specified.

You can use the scroll bars to move the photograph over the screen, and you can zoom in by opening the *View* menu and selecting *Zoom*. Select the required zoom percentage. The image is then shown on the screen as specified.

You can also use the Zoom tool to enlarge the image in steps. Select the Zoom tool and click on the left mouse button to enlarge the image and the right mouse button to reduce it. You can also use the *100%* option from the *View* menu to restore the image to its original size.

6.2 Editing photographs

Just as with CorelDRAW!, in CorelPHOTO-PAINT you have to select an object first prior to editing it. This is done by clicking on the Object Picker Tool, the black arrow corresponding to the Pick Tool provided by Corel-DRAW!. Any modifications are then applied to the selected object, and sometimes to the entire image depending on the nature of the changes. The area of the image which lies under the object normally remains intact.

The other functions in this flyout menu are used to select a certain area of the image or photograph to define it as an object. These are, from left to right: Rectangle Object Tool, Circle Object Tool, Polygon Object Tool, Freehand Object Tool, Lasso Object Tool, Magic Wand Object Tool, Object Brush Tool and Object Node Edit Tool. This last icon enables you to apply nodes to the outline of the selected object. Then you can adjust the outline to fit the required shape more easily.

Here is a summary of the functions of the tools in the toolbox:

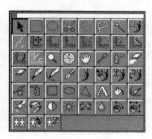

icon	function
Object Picker Tool	This selects all objects.
Rectangle Object Tool	Draws a rectangle within the image, the contents are selected.
Circle Object Tool	Draws a circle, the contents are selected.
Polygon Object Tool	Draws a polygon, its contents are selected.
Freehand Object Tool	Draws a freehand line so that irregular objects can be selected. Press the left mouse button to draw the freehand line; press the right mouse button to draw an area without a background.
Lasso Object Tool	Selects (snaps to) irregular areas with similar colour.
Magic Wand Object Tool	Selects areas with the same colours. This colour sense is defined in the *Special* menu, using the *Color Tolerance* option. You can determine the colour range yourself.
Object Brush Tool	This determines the shape of the brush. When you have selected the area (the shape), you can use the *Create Brush* option from the *Special* menu to make a new brush.
Object Node Edit Tool	You can use the Node Edit Tool to modify objects by editing their

	nodes. When you have selected an area and have clicked on the tool, the nodes are added to the selection frame.
Mask Picker Tool	Select this tool to select a predefined area. You can move, reduce, stretch and distort a mask. An image may contain only one mask.
Rectangle Mask Tool	This tool is used to select rectangular masks in an image.
Circle Mask Tool	This tool selects circular masks in an image.
Polygon Mask Tool	This tool selects multi-sided figures in an image.
Freehand Mask Tool	This tool selects irregular masks in an image.
Lasso Mask Tool	This tool is used to select irregular and similarly-coloured masks in an image.
Magic Wand Mask Tool	This is used to define masks with similar colours.
Mask Brush Tool	This determines the brush shape for selected masks.
Mask Node Edit Tool	You can use this tool to modify shapes by editing their nodes. When you have selected a mask area and then click on this tool, nodes are added to the selection frame.
Zoom Tool	The Zoom Tool enables you to enlarge and reduce the image on the screen.
Locator Tool	This tool is used to look for the same element in two or more windows.
Hand Tool	This tool is used to move the photograph or the selected area diagonally, horizontally or vertically.

Eyedropper Tool	This tool enables you to select a colour from an image. Clicking on the left mouse button selects the foreground colour, the right mouse button selects the background colour.
Local Undo Tool	This tool undoes the last action executed by the drawing tools. The shape and the area are determined by the shape and the width specified for this tool via the *Tool Settings* roll-up menu (*View* menu).
Eraser	This is used to remove specific areas from an image.
Color Replacer Tool	This tool is used to replace the primary colour with the secondary colour. The Outline and Fill colour are selected by means of the *Color* roll-up menu (*View* menu).
Line Tool	The Line Tool enables you to draw single and joined lines.
Curve Tool	The Curve Tool enables you to draw single and joined curves.
Pen Tool	The Pen Tool enables you to draw freehand shapes.
Paint Brush Tool	This tool colours an area with the selected colour. The shape and colour of the brush are determined in the *Color* roll-up menu (from the *View* menu).
Impressionism Brush Tool	This tool enables you to make brushstrokes similar to those used in impressionist painting. The brushstrokes consist of a number of preselected similar coloured lines (a red hue for example). The coloured lines are positioned on top of one another.

Pointillism Brush Tool	This tool applies points of colour, just as in the pointillistic school of painting.
Artist Brush Tool	This tool applies an existing brush style in the selected colour. Each brushstroke is a grey-tinted bitmap, 64 pixels wide and 128 pixels high (Windows BMP file). The black part indicates the transparent section, the middle grey tints are the brushstrokes and the white surfaces are the 'over-exposed' areas of the stroke. Select the colour in the *Color* roll-up menu (from the *View* menu).
AirBrush Tool	This tool sprays a layer of colour on the image.
Spraycan Tool	This tool enables you to spontaneously splatter preselected colour.
Rectangle Tool	This tool enables you to draw rectangles with or without filling, and rounded rectangles. If you hold down the Ctrl key while dragging a rectangle, a perfect square is drawn.
Ellipse Tool	This tool enables you to draw circles and oval shapes. If you hold down the Ctrl key while using this tool, a perfect circle is drawn.
Polygon Tool	This tool draws multi-sided figures, with or without filling.
Text Tool	This tool adds text to an image.
Fill Tool	This tool enables you to fill closed areas with predefined colours.
Smear Tool	This tool enables you to smear colour across an image. This resembles daubing colour on an oil painting.

Smudge Tool — This tool mixes chosen points in a selected area. This corresponds to mixing colours with crayons or pastel colours.

Sharpen Tool — This tool sharpens the elements of the selected area.

Contrast Tool — Use this tool to make areas lighter or darker. The higher the value, the more intense the colour and darker the dark areas. Lower values temper the colours.

Brightness Tool — This tool is used to alter the brightness of colours in selected areas. The colours are only changed the first time that you apply the brush.

Tint Tool — This tool allocates a selected colour to an area. This colour is applied on top of the existing colour in the image. Select the colour in the *Color* roll-up menu (*View* menu).

Blend Tool — This tool enables you to blend colours in the image. The effect is similar to that of mixing aquarel colours with water. The higher the value, the greater the blending.

Hue Tool — This tool applies a tint to an image. When you move this tool across the image, the colours are altered according to the value specified by the slide control buttons in the *Tool Settings* roll-up menu.

Saturation Tool — This tool defines the amount of grey in the image. You can select the brush used, the shape and the size from the *Tool Settings* roll-up menu. The Saturation slide control bar determines the grey value.

Clone Tool

This tool enables you to (partially or wholly) replace one area of an image by another. First click on the tool and then open the *Tool Settings* roll-up menu to define the shape, size, transparency and orientation of the clone. Click on the area to be cloned and move to the area where the clone is to be placed. Click again. The selected area is cloned. Moving the frame copies the area under the cross.

Impressionism Clone Tool

This tool reproduces a section of an image at a new position. Impressionistic brushstrokes in the same colour as the original are used. Moving the frame specifies an area; the area under the cross is reproduced. The size of the brushstrokes depends on the settings in the *Tool Settings* roll-up menu.

Pointillism Clone Tool

This tool reproduces an area of an image at a new position. Pointillistic brushstrokes are used for this reproduction, in the same colours as used in the original. The size of the points depends on the settings in the *Tool Settings* roll-up menu.

We advise you to experiment with all these facilities. The illustration opposite shows a photograph with increased contrast of two monkeys after a visit to Carnaby St.

6.3 Filter functions

Many improvements to photographs consist of retouching mistakes, accentuating contrasts and applying special effects. CorelPHOTO-PAINT provides various filter functions for implementing these kinds of actions. They are available in the *Effects* menu. Click on one of the filters in this menu to view the various interconnected filters. Select one of these filters and try out some of the settings in the corresponding dialog window.

We shall demonstrate the effects of the various filters using the same photograph each time so that you can get an idea of the different possibilities. This photograph can be found under the name FLOWERS2.TIF on Disk1 of the CD ROM set, in the CLIPART_BITMAPS\TEXTURES directory. It is advisable to examine the modifications by means of the Preview button wherever possible, before actually applying the changes.

You can use the *Undo* command from the *Edit* menu to remove the filter effect (as long as you have not made other changes in the meantime).

Artistic

Pointillism
This filter displays the image in individual points. The effect can be subtle, while the character of the original remains. You can also vary the points and the colours to produce more extravagant effects.

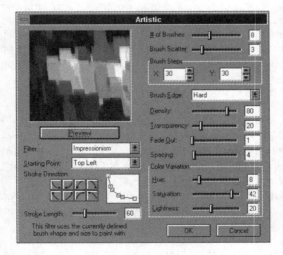

Impressionism
The Impressionism filter gives the image the appearance of an oil painting. You can apply a minimal effect, or

change the brush shape, the length and thickness of the brushstrokes, the number of brushes and the colours, if you want to change the image more thoroughly. Select a small area of the image and experiment with this filter. Processing the image is rather time-consuming. This filter is very suitable for large bold objects; applying it to vague photographs can be a bit disappointing.

Color

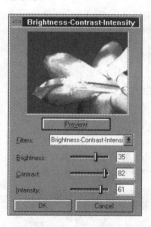

Brightness and Contrast
Use this filter to make an image lighter or darker, and to alter the dividing line between lightness and darkness.

Gamma
Use this filter to improve details in an image. To do this, define the middle grey tints without changing shadow and light areas.

Hue/Saturation

Set this filter without changing the brightness. The hue refers to a special colour, such as red or green. The saturation refers to the intensity of this colour.

Tone Map

This filter enables you to apply colour corrections and special filters in one or more colour channels.

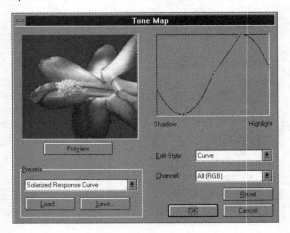

Fancy

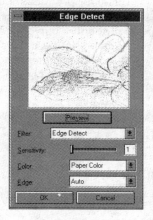

Edge Detect

This filter applies special out-lining effects to an image. You can specify the Sensitivity, the Color and the Edge to vary the effect.

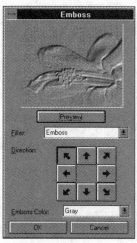

Emboss

Emboss creates a three-dimensional effect. The arrows indicate the direction of the incoming light and thus determine the angle of light and shadow. The selected colour determines the basic image colour.

Gaussian Blur

This filter produces a hazy effect. The name refers to the bell-shaped curve generated by mapping the colour values of the pixels in the image. The higher the radius number, the greater the blurring.

Invert

This filter inverts the colours in the image.

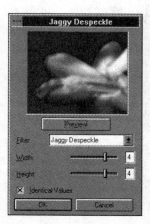

Jaggy Despeckle

This filter spreads the colours in an image. The image then becomes softer and more vague.

Motion Blur

This effect simulates motion. The arrows indicate the direction of the motion.

Outline

This filter gives an outline to selected objects or images. Objects with solid colour are outlined with the colour of that object. The insides of objects and the background areas of the image are filled with a grey colour.

Mapping

Glass Block

The Glass block filter displays the image as if it were situated behind a plate glass pane.

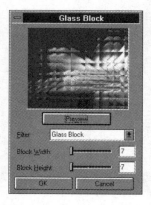

Impressionist

This filter applies an impressionistic style to the image.

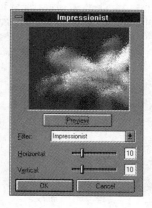

Map to Sphere
This effect wraps the image around various forms.

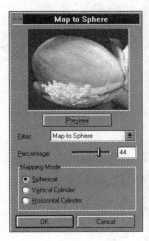

Pinch/Punch
When you apply this effect, it appears as if the centre of the image has been pressed in or pulled out.

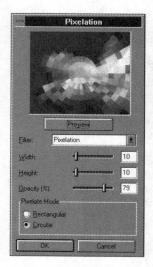

Pixelate

Applying this effect results in a circular or rectangular display. Specify the size of the pixel blocks (Width and Height) and the opacity in the dialog window.

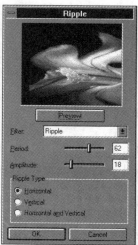

Ripple

The Ripple filter can distort the image in vertical and horizontal waves. Specify the relevant settings to reach the required effect.

Smoked Glass

The Smoked Glass filter places a transparent dark filter over the image.

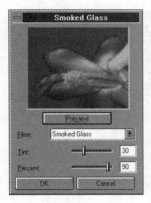

Swirl

Select a high factor to increase the rotation. The object rotates around the midpoint of the image.

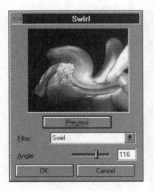

Tile

Tiling produces a pattern which gives many smaller versions of the original image.

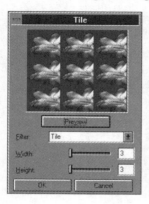

Vignette

This filter places a round, opaque mask around the image; the middle of the image remains visible. You can also determine the colour of the mask.

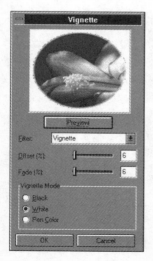

Wet Paint

This option produces an optical effect as if the paint on the image is not yet dry. Specify the Percentage for the depth of the paint; a low value makes it look like the paint is only laid on the surface.

Wind

If you apply the Wind filter, it looks like wind is blowing across the image.

Noise

Add Noise

This filter produces a granular effect to an image that is too flat or overly blended.

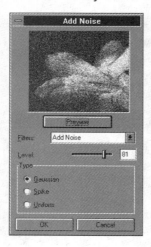

Maximum

This filter makes an image lighter. The pixel values are adjusted to decrease the number of colours.

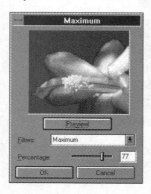

Median
This filter removes the granularity from scanned images which tend to look rather course.

Minimum
This filter makes an image darker by adjusting the pixel values to decrease the number of colours.

Remove Noise
This filter softens outlines and removes irregularities which occur during scanning. All pixels are set to an average value based on the values of the surrounding pixels.

Sharpen

Adaptive Unsharp
This filter places the emphasis on details at the edges without altering the rest of the image. This produces particularly clear effects with colour images with high resolution.

Directional Sharpen

This filter analyses pixel values in various directions to determine in which direction the highest sharpening factor can be applied.

Edge Enhance

This effect accentuates edges in areas with various colours and patterns.

Enhance
Use this filter to accentuate or smoothen edges.

Sharpen
This filter increases the resolution sharpness of the image or selected area.

Unsharp Mask
This filter accentuates the details at the edges and sharpens the smooth areas in the image.

Soften

Diffuse
The Diffuse filter spreads colour so that the image looks hazy.

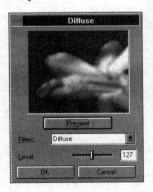

Directional Smooth

With the Directional Smooth filter, the value of similarly-coloured pixels is analysed to determine in which direction the greatest smoothing should take place.

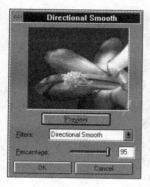

Smooth

The Smooth filter reduces the difference between adjacent pixels. This restricts loss of detail and the image or selected object is equalized.

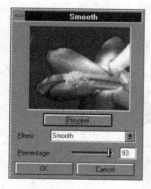

Soften
The Soften filter changes the contrast. Extreme contrasts are tempered by softening the colours or grey tints.

Special

Contour
This filter applies a contour to the edges of an image.

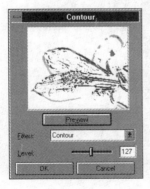

Posterize

This filter removes gradations so that areas with solid colours and grey tints are produced. The lower the value, the more powerful the effect.

Psychedelic

This filter produces a brightly coloured version of the image.

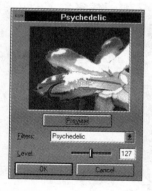

Solarize

This filter will produce a complementary version of the image. You can determine the extent of this yourself.

Threshold

This filter gradually lightens an image.

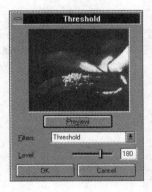

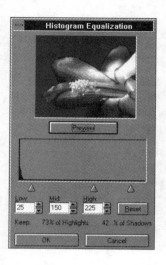

Tone

Equalize

This filter uses a histogram to redistribute shades of colours. The darkest colours are made black, the lightest white and the other colours range between these. It is often best to equalize a scanned image first before applying other filters.

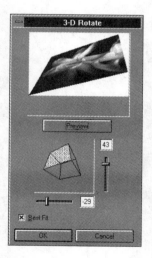

Transformations

3D Rotate

Use the vertical and horizontal levers to rotate the image in the window.

Mesh Warp

The image can be changed by dragging the mesh inter-sections to a different position. The size of the mesh can also be adjusted.

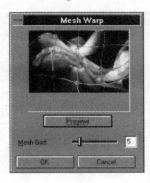

Perspective

This filter enables you to transform the image by drag-ging the corner handles towards or away from the mid-dle.

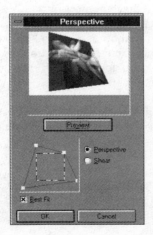

6.4   Printing and saving images

When you have edited a photograph, you can print it by
means of the *Print* command from the *File* menu.

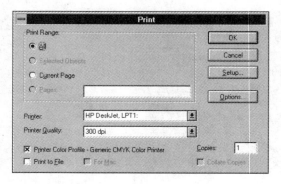

Specify in the Print Range section whether you wish to
print all pages or only the current page. If you have selected objects, you can print only these by clicking on
the Selected Objects option button. You can use the
Pages option to determine which range of pages or individual pages you wish to have printed.

Specify the Printer you wish to use to print the selected
page(s) or objects. The Printer Quality defines the required resolution. The drop-down list in this section only
displays the actual printer capabilities.

Specify the number of copies required in the Copies
section. Click on OK when you are satisfied with the settings.

If you wish to save an image, open the *File* menu and select *Save*. If the modified photograph has already been
allocated a name, the file will be updated to save the
most recent alterations. If you wish to use a different

name for the file, or save it as a different type of file, select the *Save As* command. Type the required name in the subsequent dialog window and specify the appropriate drive and directory for the file. Click on OK to confirm the command. With very large files, it is advisable to save the file as a Compressed file in the File Sub-Format section. This will save disk space.

7 CorelSHOW - Creating presentations

The CorelDRAW! package provides a program which enables you to present images and charts in a professional way: CorelSHOW. We shall discuss the possibilities of creating and editing your own screen presentations. You can, for example, use CorelSHOW to make a professional photographical presentation of your company.

In addition, we shall deal with the multi-media aspect in which we shall demonstrate how to create simple multimedial presentations with CorelSHOW.

The program is based on the OLE technique. This is an abbreviation of *Object Linking and Embedding*. This makes it possible to combine various Windows applications so that you can easily copy and link data, or combine texts, pictures, photographs, charts and cartoon trickery to form a single file.

The so-called objects (texts, images, sound) are created in their own applications and are then transferred to a special program. This special program manages the objects and is capable of presenting them as required. This program can be a desktop publishing program for instance. In this, texts and pictures are combined to form a document which is then printed. CorelSHOW is a presentation program which is also capable of combining and presenting objects from various sources. Speeches and discussions can be given graphical support, making it more interesting for the listeners. This OLE technique provides all sorts of possibilities for creating presentations. Once the presentation has been created, you can copy it as many times as you wish and pass it on to the audience or the customers. In short, we imagine this presentation to be run either automatically or manually on the PC, supported by the spoken word or by music.

The topics in this chapter:
• what are multi-media applications?
• starting up and closing down CorelSHOW
• making OLE links
• inserting animations
• defining the effects and the duration
• copying and distributing presentations.

7.1 What are multi-media applications?

The term *multi-media* appears on all street corners these days. Hardware suppliers praise their wares as being multi-media PCs. Software suppliers claim that it is possible to apply their programs in a multi-medial way. What does this all mean?

A good definition is something like: A technique of application in which text, sound and images are (can be) integrated. Comparison with television programs may be useful here. Television fulfills the audiovisual criteria mentioned above, but the informative value of many television programs is often less than zero. Some programs, such as documentaries and current affairs programs, do present worthwhile information but there is no *interaction* with the viewer. By this, we mean that the viewer is not able to interrupt the program in order to ask a question or to clarify an aspect. New developments seem to indicate that the day that this will actually occur is not too distant. In the meantime, the computer, especially via the Internet, provides more possibilities than the television.

With computers, interaction depends on the software and thus on the creativity of the programmers. The hardware functions only as a platform, in the same way as a television provides a good picture and clear sound.

Almost all computers nowadays have a colour monitor. If you acquire a sound card and loudspeakers, you have a basic multi-media set. You can add a number of elements to this, such as a CD ROM drive (double speed is the best) and a graphic video overlay card for editing digital video sequences.

However, the software that makes use of this hardware is of far more importance to the user.

Video conferences, presentation, advertising and educational programs all make use of multi-medial applications nowadays. In addition, multi-medial applications are also to be found in office communication and, increasingly, on the consumer market. The latter promises to be an explosive field of development in the near future.

These applications will be indispensible in a few years. Each computer book will contain a diskette which will produce the entire book on the screen. But not as normal text; it will contain video clips with instructions from the author on how to operate the programs. You will be able to ask questions via the keyboard and the answer will be given immediately.

7.2 Starting up CorelSHOW

Below, we shall outline an example of a small presentation in order to give an impression of the various facilities available. First, start up the program by double clicking on the CorelSHOW icon in the Corel group window. Then open the *File* menu and select *New*.

To create a new presentation, you first have to specify a number of slides and then click on OK. You can always add more slides later if required. We have specified three for our example. The CorelSHOW working area then appears.

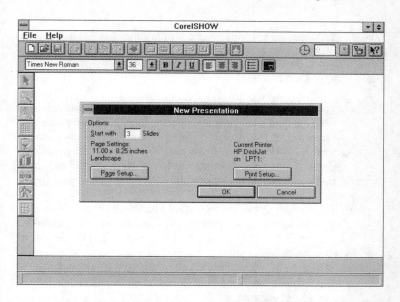

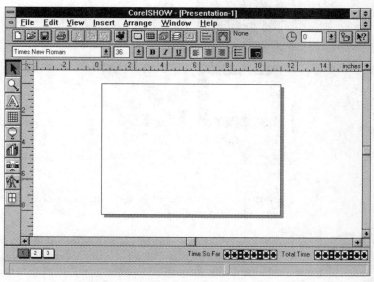

The familiar toolbox is shown flanking the left-hand side of the screen. This toolbox also enables you to switch quickly to other programs which support the OLE technique.

The fourth icon from the top, the Background Library, enables you to construct a background. Sample files are supplied along with the package and these are copied to the harddisk during the installation. There are more sample backgrounds available on the CD. To select a background, proceed as follows:

1) Click on the Background Library icon.
2) Select a library with background files, such as SAM-PLES.SHB in the \SHOW\BACKGRDS directory on the CD.

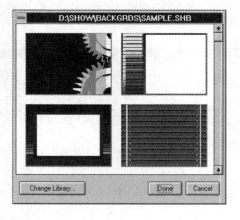

3) Click on a suitable background and close the window by clicking on Done.

If you wish to use a background from a different library, click on the Change Library button. Select a different file from a different directory in the subsequent dialog window. Once a background has been selected, it will be used for every picture in the presentation so that the layout will give a uniform impression.

7.3 Creating the OLE link

To create pictures, an OLE link with a different program has to be made, since it is not possible to create images using CorelSHOW. To do so, make use of the small icons in the toolbox. The balloon will activate Corel-DRAW!. The chart icon will activate CorelCHART. If you click on the small window at the bottom of the row, the *Insert Object* dialog window is opened, enabling you to switch over to other programs that are installed on the computer.

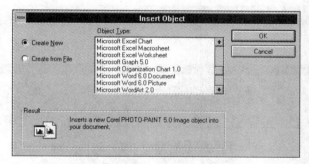

The figure shows that it is possible to make links with Excel, Word and WordArt among others. Double click on the name of the required program to switch to it.

For our own particular example, we shall begin with the opening welcome picture for the presentation. We shall create a link with CorelDRAW!. Click on the balloon icon. When you release the mouse button, CorelDRAW! will be displayed on the screen.

Type the text as shown in the figure below and choose a ClipArt drawing to accompany the text.

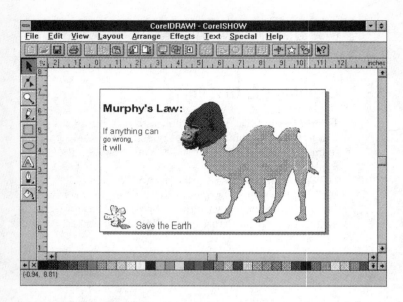

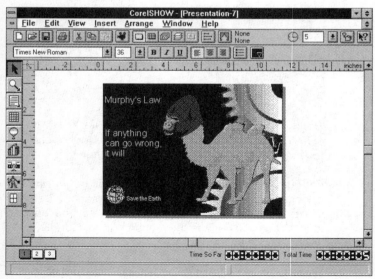

We have compiled different images and have used yellow letters to stand out against the dark background.

When you have completed your drawing, open the *File* menu and select *Exit & Return to CorelSHOW*. Answer Yes to the subsequent question. The opening screen is now ready.

As you see the CorelDRAW! image is fitted neatly into the predefined window. You can still alter the size and position of the image. To do so, click on the object and drag the mouse to the new position, or drag one of the handles until the object acquires the necessary size.

The other slides in the presentation are made in the same way. First activate a new empty page by clicking on the page number 2 button in the bottom left-hand corner of the screen. Then select the Chart icon in the toolbox to create a link to CorelCHART. We have chosen a simple line diagram. Make any specifications in the diagram (via the worksheet) and when you are satisfied, open the *File* menu and select *Exit & Return to CorelSHOW*.

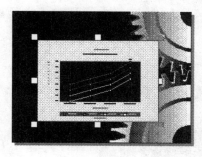

On the third page of the presentation, we shall demonstrate how to make a link with a program which is not a component of the CorelDRAW! standard package. Select the small window icon at the bottom of the toolbox.

The subsequent dialog window displays all the programs which are able to be linked to CorelSHOW. For instance, if you have Word for Windows on your computer, the dialog window will show the WordArt program. We shall activate this program. Proceed as above to create the third slide. Type a text of your choice. Select a light colour from the Color section if your text is to be placed on a dark background.

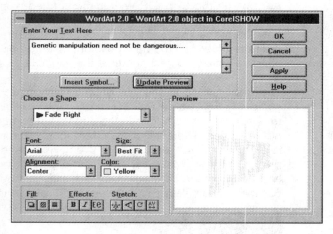

Click on OK to transfer the newly-created object to CorelSHOW.

You can, of course, experiment with other objects. Video and sound effects can give particularly interesting results. There are a number of sample files on the Corel CD Sampler (WAV files) in the SOUNDS directory. You can make use of the *Sound* option from the *Insert* menu to integrate a sound file in the presentation.

Our small presentation consisting of three slides is now complete. If you want an idea of what this looks like, you can start it up. This is done by clicking on the Run Screen Show button (the film projector) on the standard toolbar. Answer Yes to the subsequent question and the screen show will begin.

7.4 Specifying the playing time and adding special effects

Finally, the separate pictures should be attached to one another in some way. This means that you have to determine the length of time each slide is to be displayed and you have to specify the transition effects. There are icons at the top of the window which will perform these functions quickly and easily.

The Transition Effect button enables you to determine various sorts of progressions. Click on the button to open the corresponding dialog window. Select the required option for the currently active slide. Activate another slide by clicking on the relevant page number button at the bottom of the screen. You can examine the effect by clicking on the Preview button or by actually running the screen show (film projector icon).

You determine the length of time the slide is to be shown by opening the Time On-screen list (next to the clock) and specifying the number of seconds; you can also simply type the required number in the text box next to the clock.

The right length of display time is important, but also difficult to determine. Images which are too short or too long do not convey the message. Reading the text on the slides aloud will give an indication of the length of time they should be shown.

There are two digital time measuring instruments at the lower right-hand part of the screen. The time taken up until the current slide is shown behind Time So Far; the total duration of the presentation is shown behind Total Time. Accordingly, you can keep an eye on the relative duration of each slide.

The Timelines function also provides a manner of checking the duration and also enables you to operate the individual slide processes. The function is activated by clicking on the Timelines icon (next to the curtains).

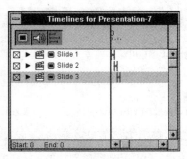

The separate pages of the presentation are shown underneath one another. The duration of each is shown at the right-hand side by means of the green bars. The duration of the slide show is represented by the small stripes above the green bars.

You can alter the duration of each slide by dragging the bars to the right or the left. You can also determine this for each slide, sound effect or specified object separately if necessary. Click on the triangular arrow to do so.

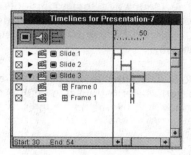

The check boxes next to the slides enable you to activate or deactivate one or more of the objects or even the entire slide.

7.5 Sorting the slides

When the presentation has been completed, you can change the order of sequence of the slides if you wish. This takes place in the Slide Sorter View mode, to which you can switch by clicking on the button displaying the three sheets of paper on the Standard toolbar.

Select one of the slides by clicking on it. The order of sequence is altered by moving the mouse pointer to it and then dragging it to a new position. You can delete an image by selecting it and pressing the Del key. You can insert one or more new slides by selecting this option from the *Insert* menu. Specify the number of new slides and their position in relation to the existing slides in the subsequent dialog window.

It is also possible to insert animations into the presentation. There are several samples available on the CD. We shall deal with moving pictures in chapter 9, Corel-MOVE.

7.6   Passing on the presentation

Once a presentation has been created, it can be run on any computer on which CorelSHOW has been installed. The Corel package also contains a runtime version of CorelSHOW.

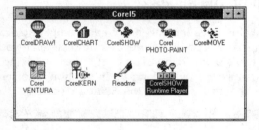

You can pass on this program to everyone, along with the presentation, since it is a public domain program that can be copied legally. The recipient of the presentation only needs to start up the runtime version and open the file in order to be able to view the presentation. In order to have your presentation shown using the Corel-SHOW PLAYER, you have to save the presentation as a file with the extension .SHR.

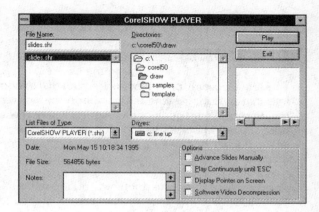

As the figure shows, the runtime version provides several options for displaying the presentation. For instance, you can determine whether or not the slide advance should take place manually or automatically and whether the show should go on until the Esc key is pressed.

It is not possible to save these presentations in Corel-SHOW PLAYER.

Presentations containing animation files are dealt with in a different way. In order to show a presentation with video or animation sequences, the CorelMOVE program, or another animation program (such as AutoDesk Animator, QuickTime for Windows), has to be installed on the computer. Otherwise only a bitmap image will appear on the screen.

8 CorelDRAW! - Utility programs

There are several programs in the CorelDRAW! package that perform routine tasks in order to facilitate the creation and management of images. One of these programs, CorelMOSAIC has the function of managing existing drawings: printing, deleting, searching for files etc.

Another recurring procedure involved in the creation of images is the conversion of pixel-based images to vector-based images. If, for example, you have created images in Paintbrush or CorelPAINT and want to edit them further in CorelDRAW!, these drawings first have to be converted to vector format. The CorelTRACE program enables you to do this.

CorelQUERY enables you to load and sort existing tables from Access or dBASE.

Topics dealt with in this chapter:
- opening CorelMOSAIC
- making a link to other programs
- an overview of the CorelMOSAIC menus
- converting bitmap images to vector-based images
- creating tables using CorelQUERY

8.1 CorelMOSAIC

CorelMOSAIC can be regarded as a visual file manager. The great virtue of this program is that it allows you to examine images in advance and subsequently start up the relevant editing application.

Start up CorelMOSAIC by double clicking on the icon in the Corel5 group window. Open the *File* menu and se-

lect *Open Collection.* Select the \CLIPART_BIT-
MAPS\FANTASY directory on the first laser disk.

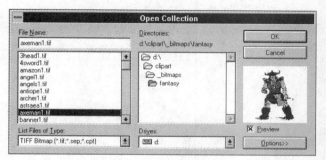

Confirm your choice by clicking on OK. CorelMOSAIC
provides an overview of all the images that it automatically recognises and that can be edited using one of the
Corel programs.

Double click on one of the pictures. CorelMOSAIC automatically opens the corresponding program, such as CorelPHOTO-PAINT for example.

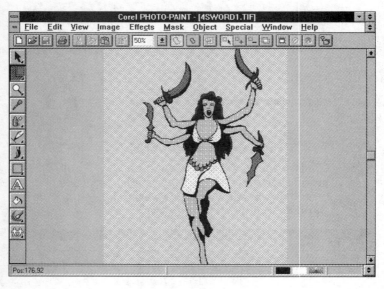

As you know, Windows enables you to work with various programs simultaneously. For instance, imagine that CorelPHOTO-PAINT is currently active; you can switch back to CorelMOSAIC by pressing Alt+Tab. The program you have just left remains resident in the background and can be easily reactivated by pressing Alt+Tab once more. In this way, you can use CorelMOSAIC to manage the pictures and to make links to the other Corel applications. Accordingly, pictures can easily be found, edited, printed or deleted. These actions, along with others, are performed by means of the menu commands.

8.1.1   The File menu

The *File* menu contains eleven options.

New Collection
This option enables you to create a new collection, in other words, a main file for saving miniatures (so-called thumbnails) or for archiving files. It is only possible to create libraries and catalogues in CorelMOSAIC; it is not possible to create directories.

When you select a catalogue, the main file contains thumbnail sketches and references to files, but not the actual files themselves. The archived versions of the original files are stored in a library.

Open Collection
Specify the directory path to the required graphic files in the *Open Collection* dialog window. Enter the type of file you are looking for in the List Files of Type box. It is advisable to specify All Files here so that CorelMOSAIC will also provide access to types of files such as PCX and BMP as well as Corel files.

If you wish to look for pictures by means of certain keywords, click on the Options button.

Delete Collection

This command enables you to delete a catalogue or library which you have created yourself. You cannot delete directories in CorelMOSAIC.

If you delete a library, the relevant files are also deleted. If, in contrast, you delete a catalogue, only the stored references are deleted; the files themselves remain intact.

Convert

This option opens a dialog window enabling you to convert pictures to various different file types. Click on OK once you have made a choice and have specified a location for the converted file.

If you convert files from earlier versions of CorelDRAW! or CorelCHART, the relevant programs are used in the conversion process. This means that the corresponding program must be installed on your computer. The application runs in the background during the conversion.

Use CorelTRACE to convert bitmap files to vector-based files. If you wish to convert the file type of a number of files, those files which CorelMOSAIC does not support will simply be ignored. A message box appears subsequent to the conversion process, giving information about the unconverted files.

Print Files

Select this option to print one or more of the files in the overview. You should first select the picture by clicking on it. You can select several pictures in one go by holding down the Shift or the Ctrl key while clicking on them one by one. If you then select *Print Files* from the *File* menu, CorelMOSAIC will open the graphic program to print the graphic files. If you click on the Options button in the *print* dialog window, you can specify special print settings in the *Print Options* dialog window. Click on OK to start the print procedure.

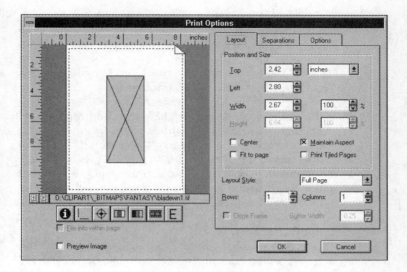

Print Thumbnails

This option enables you to print an overview of the selected pictures. Make sure that you activate the Selected Objects option button in the Print Range section.

Print Setup

This option enables you to select the printer to specify special print options.

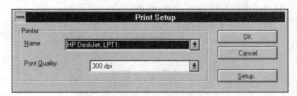

Color Manager

The Color Manager enables you to create a system profile based on the monitor, scanner and printer being used. This profile then enables Corel applications to adopt, display and print colours on various devices more exactly.

The system colour profile guarantees that

- the colours displayed on the screen correspond as accurately as possible to those printed;
- the photographs and colours that are part of images are passed on to the printer as precisely as possible;
- the scanner colours as adjusted in such a way that they correspond to those on the scanned image as much as possible.

Color Correction
This option enables you to improve the accuracy of the example on the screen. The screen build-up is retarded a little when bitmaps are being examined.

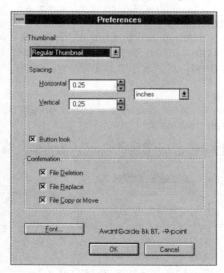

Preferences
The *Preferences* option opens a dialog window (see the previous page) in which you can determine how to preview the images on the screen.

In addition, you can specify which font is to be used for thumbnail labels and whether or not confirmation is necessary for deleting, moving and copying files.

Exit
This command closes down the CorelMOSAIC program.

8.1.2 The Edit menu

The *Edit* menu contains five groups of options. The commands in this menu enable you to remove, edit, import and export images.

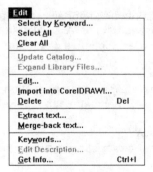

Select by Keyword, Select All, Clear All
If you want to select one, several or all of the images, select one of these commands. If keywords have been allocated to image files, you can make a selection based on one or more selection criteria. The *Clear All* option may be a bit misleading: the *selection* of one or more images is undone, the images remain available for further selection if required.

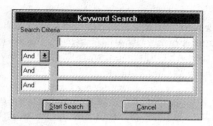

Update Catalog

This command updates thumbnails and file information when modifications are made to a file in the catalog.

Expand Library Files

This command expands one or more archived, selected files from the library and places it in the required directory. You can only edit files from the library when they have been expanded. All expanded files are stored in the same directory.

Catalogues can only contain thumbnails and references to the location of the original file. Accordingly, it is not possible to expand a library file into a catalogue.

Edit

Activate this command to open the application that belongs to the selected file. The image can then be edited.

Import into CorelDRAW!

This command opens an existing drawing in Corel-DRAW!.

Delete

This command deletes one or more files.

Extract text

This command converts text from a selected graphic file to an ASCII file. You can subsequently edit this text using an editor.

Merge-back text
This command places texts which have been extracted for editing in an ASCII file back into CorelDRAW! files.

Keywords
This option enables you to add, or to remove, keywords to selected files.

Edit Description
This option enables you to modify a string of characters that were assigned to a catalogue when it was created. This description can have a maximum length of 128 characters and can be printed along with the thumbnail sketches. You can only edit a catalogue description when the catalogue is actually opened.

Get Info
This option enables you to display an image in large format along with detailed information such as the file size, the date of creation and the assigned keywords.

8.2 CorelTRACE

The CorelTRACE program makes it possible to convert pixel-based images into vector-based images. Pixel-based images have the disadvantage that they tend to become vague and angled when they are enlarged. In contrast, vector programs create sharp and even contours that can be enlarged, reduced and rotated as required. Moreover, vector-based images occupy less disk space.

The conversion process takes places as follows. Coherent areas in a pixel-based image are copied in such a way that all the important elements become available as objects for further modification in a vector-based image. This copying method is referred to as *tracing*. The imag-

es which are to be converted may come from digital
scanners, drawing and photograph processing programs such as Paintbrush and CorelPHOTO-PAINT and
bitmap cliparts such as screen shots made using Hijaak
or Hotshot. The figure below shows an example of a converted file.

We shall give an example of the conversion of a pixel-
based image of the TIF file type to a vector-based format.
First start up the CorelTRACE program. The opening
screen appears (see the opposite page).

Now open the pixel-based image you wish to convert, by
selecting *Open* from the *File* menu. Select the pixel type
from the List Files of Type drop-down list. That can be
TIF, PCX or BMP files for example. Specify the required
drive and directory. Then click on the required file name.
If the Preview check box is activated, the chosen image
will be shown in the sample box in the dialog window.
Confirm your choice by clicking on OK. After a few seconds, the selected pixel-based image will appear in the
left-hand window.

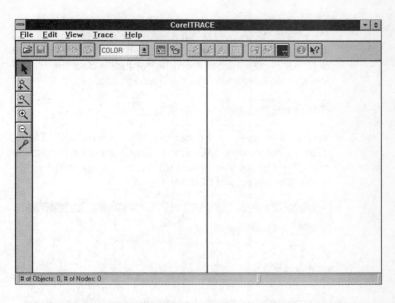

CorelTRACE provides six tracing methods. These are available in the *Trace* menu, and can also be activated by clicking on the buttons on the toolbar along the top of the screen (see *Help* menu, *Tracing buttons*).

You should specify the conversion options first. These settings determine the way in which the pixel image is converted to the vector format. To do so, open the *Trace* menu and select *Edit Options*.

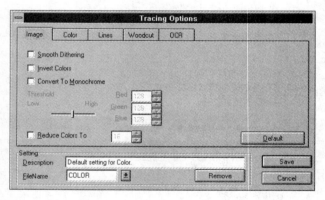

The *Tracing Options* dialog window provides options for each type of conversion. Clicking on the Save button in the Setting section at the bottom of the window will save the specifications for the chosen category. The image options enable you to regulate the precision of the conversion to the smallest detail. The greater the precision, the larger the traced file. Changes in the options influence the size and complexity of the converted file. Keep in mind that a file which is too complex may cause problems when opening it in CorelDRAW! or when trying to print it.

Each category (tabsheet) in the dialog window provides options for tracing the image. Click on these tabsheets one by one to examine the options.

You can type a description of the selected options in the Setting section and also assign a file name there. Click on the Save button to store the specified settings under the allocated name. The file is then automatically given the extension CTR. The file name is subsequently shown in the drop-down list (currently showing COLOR) on the toolbar along the top of the screen. CorelTRACE has four standard settings:

- MONO: this is the standard setting for black-and-white tracing
- COLOR: the standard setting for colour tracing
- FORM: the standard setting for the Form tracing method
- DITHERED: the standard setting for tracing an image with dithered colours (colour simulated by putting dots very lose together).

Once you have chosen a tracing option, open the *File* menu and specify the output options, including the drive and directory where the converted file is to be saved. This is done by selecting the *Save Options* command.

When you are satisfied with all the specified settings, click on the appropriate tracing button. CorelTRACE implements the conversion. Subsequently, open the *File* menu and select *Save Trace*. The file is stored with the EPS extension in the selected directory. You can now open the converted image in CorelDRAW! for further modification by selecting the *Import* option from the *File* menu. Then save the modified image under a different name with the extension CDR. This ensures that the file is always available for access by CorelDRAW!.

8.3   Searching with CorelQUERY

This utility program enables you to search for all kinds of data files from various programs, such as dBASE, Microsoft Excel and Access. CorelQUERY makes use of the Microsoft ODBC function which, of course, must be installed. We shall presume that you have indeed selected the ODBC operating program when Windows was installed.

In this section, we shall discuss the facilities provided by CorelQUERY and also demonstrate that you can use the program without Corel applications. For example, you can create tables that contain all the data from the original database or only a part of it. This function is very convenient when, for instance, you only require a copy of a certain amount of the customers in a list. Or perhaps you may want to combine data from more than one database. Using CorelQUERY, you can combine fields from several databases to form one table which you can then sort according to specified criteria.

8.3.1   An example using CorelQUERY

In this example, we shall outline how to create a query to gather data which are to be edited in CorelCHART. This kind of query consists of three stages:

- Choose the application in which the database was created.
- Specify a name for the data source you are going to create and use. You are going to store the required data here.
- Select the directory in which the original data file is stored.

Choosing the application
We presume that CorelQUERY has been started up. Open the *File* menu and select *New*. The following dialog window appears:

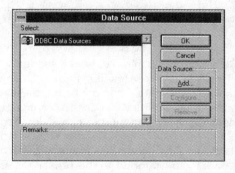

Click on the Add button to create a new data source. From the subsequent list of applications shown, select the application that was used to create the data files containing the data you want to use. We shall use Access as an example here.

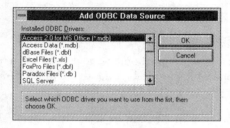

Click on OK. The *ODBC Setup for Microsoft Access* dialog window appears.

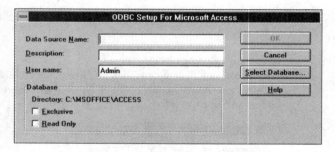

In the Data Source Name box, type a name for the file you are going to create. This file is going to be used to gather the required data. Then click on the Select Database button to select the database that contains the required data. Click on OK when you have done so.

The *Data Source* dialog window is opened. You will see that the name you assigned to the new file is shown in the list. Select this name (in our case *example*) and click on OK. The *Query Builder* window appears.

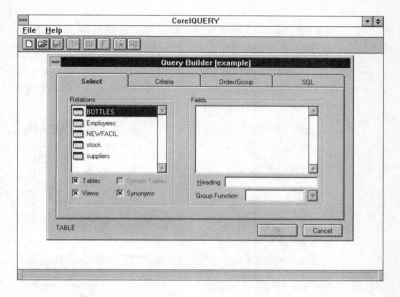

Creating the query

Double click on a table name in the Relations list to select the corresponding fields. The fields are then shown
in the list at the right-hand side. If you click on several
names in the left-hand list, the fields in these tables are
also selected. In this way, you can combine fields from
various tables.

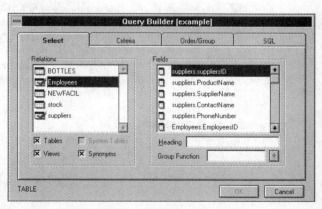

Select the fields you require by double clicking on them
in the right-hand list. The selected fields are indicated by
a red tick mark. You can assign a new name to each of
the selected fields in the Heading box. This is done by
double clicking on the field name and then changing the
text in the Heading box.

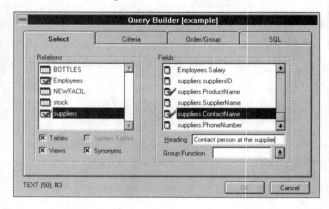

Restricting the data range

When a new table is created, all the data in the selected
fields are displayed. If you wish to limit the query by further selection, click on the Criteria tabsheet.

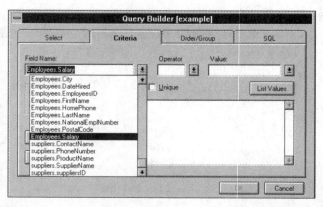

Select a field from the Field Name list. Open the Operator list and select a logical selection criterion, such as the Less Than sign. Then specify a value in the Value box. You can also open a list of the values which belong to the field selected in the Field Name list. This is done by clicking on the List Values button and opening the Value drop-down list. Click on the appropriate value.

When you click on the Add button, the specified query is summarised in the query section.

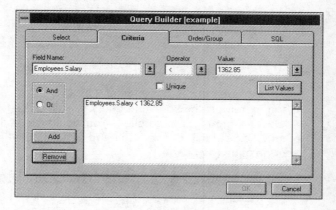

Order/Group

You can determine the sorting order for your data on the Order/Group tabsheet. Select a field and specify the sorting method in the Order section and the function to be applied in the Function section.

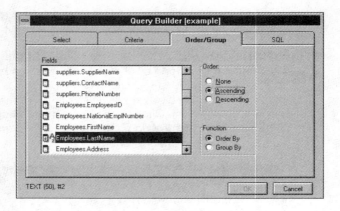

Implementing the query

Finally, open the SQL tabsheet. Click on the Build button to convert the specified query into an SQL (System Query Language) instruction. You could enter this instruction directly, but you do need to have some knowledge of this language.

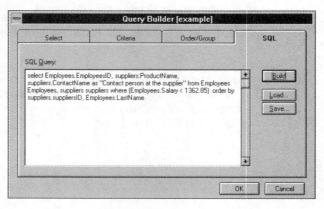

Click on the OK button to implement the query. The result is a table that you can further modify in Corel-CHART.

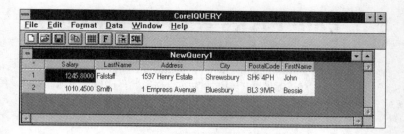

To modify the table in CorelCHART, select the entire table by clicking in the box with the asterisk in the upper left-hand corner. Then open the *Edit* menu and select *Copy*. Switch to CorelCHART and activate the worksheet. Open the *Edit* menu there and click on *Paste*. The table is inserted into the worksheet. You can now design the row and column headings as described in chapter 5.

9   Film tricks with CorelMOVE

The versatile animation program CorelMOVE enables you to make your own cartoons, animation sequences and create so-called *morphing* effects. These extras can also give your presentations more allure or convey greetings in an original way.

CorelMOVE itself is the midpoint or control centre of this process. The different images from CorelPHOTO-PAINT or CorelDRAW! are combined in CorelMOVE to become a single film. The main task consists of organising the takes, coordinating the actors, acquiring the props and recording the sound.

The topics in this chapter:

- props
- actors
- sound waves
- cues
- composing the animations
- creating the video sequences
- blending images (photographs).

9.1   The nature of films

Movement in films is, of course, pure illusion. A film consists of no more than a series of separate still pictures. By displaying these consecutively at the right speed, the idea of motion is conveyed to the viewer. This is due to the slowness of our eyes which are not able to record the rapid advance of the individual pictures. When images which resemble one another are projected in this way, the eyes record this as an ongoing movement in which the interim steps are taken for granted. Corel-MOVE works using exactly the same principle, in other words, the separate images are also shown in rapid succession.

A CorelMOVE film consists of four basic elements:

- props
- actors
- sound (wave)
- cues

You could compare a prop to a piece of stage scenery. It is stationary and can only be changed by means of blending effects. Mountains and forests in the background for example, can be regarded as props.

People and animals can move in front of this scenery. These are the *actors*, who are also composed of a number of separate images. The actors account for the actual movement in the film. Their speed depends on the number of images CorelMOVE can reproduce on the screen per second. If the image of an actor remains roughly the same throughout a number of individual film fragments, the motion is shown slower because it takes time to process the large number of images. The smaller the distance of movement between the images, the slower and more harmonic the movement.

The third element in a CorelMOVE film is *sound*.

The three elements mentioned are eventually combined to form a whole. You specify, for example, which sound or piece of music should be played when a background or an actor appears or disappears.

The fourth element in CorelMOVE is the cue. This enables you to operate the animation interactively. You can intervene in the course of the animation by pressing a key or clicking on the mouse in order to place a certain cue.

Although you can make use of any number of props, actors and sound waves, keep in mind that too many of these will retard the playing speed.

We shall now use an example to demonstrate the kinds of results you can achieve with CorelMOVE.

9.2   Starting up CorelMOVE

Double click on the CorelMOVE icon in the Corel5 group window under Program Manager. Initially, an application window is shown with only the *File* and *Help* menus available. Open the *File* menu, select *New* and enter a name for the new file. Click on OK.

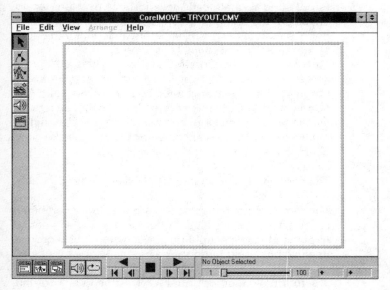

The operating panel is situated along the bottom of the screen with the buttons for the Timelines, the Library and the Cel Order. The other buttons on the operating panel largely correspond to those on a video recorder. You can use these to start up and stop the animation and to wind it forwards and backwards. The sound button switches the sound on and off. The Loop button enables you to repeat the animation any number of times.

The Status Bar, currently showing 'No Object Selected', gives information about the type and the name of an object or actor. The slide control bar indicates the current position of a running animation in the program. You can use this bar to move quickly to another position in the animation.

The toolbox is situated at the left-hand flank of the screen. It provides the following functions, from top to bottom:

- Pick Tool to select objects
- Path Tool to select actors and create paths
- Actor Tool to create new actors
- Prop Tool to create new props
- Sound Tool to create new sounds
- Cue Tool to create new cues, in other words, to determine the beginning of a new sequence.

The application window is chiefly occupied by the *animation window*. This is the working area where the animation is put together. The menu bar is situated along the top of the window as usual.

We shall begin with a short film sequence in which a spaceship is flying through space. The images required for this are available on the CDs from the Corel package. You can also adopt background sounds from the SOUNDS directory on one of the laser disks. But you can also add your own sounds by means of a microphone and a sound card.

9.3   The background

One prop will occupy the entire background in our short
example. Open the *File* menu and select *New*. Enter a
name for the animation, preferably one which gives an indication of the contents or one which rolls off the tongue
in case you reach Hollywood. Click on OK. The Corel-
MOVE animation window appears. Open the *Library* roll-
up menu by selecting this option from the *View* menu or
by clicking on the Library button at the bottom left-hand
side of the screen. In the figure we have opened the roll-
up menu by clicking on the button.

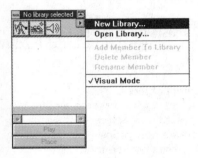

Click on the arrow pointing right at the top of the roll-up.
Click on the *Open Library* option. Select a library from
the \MOVE\LIBRARY directory on the second laser
disk. In our example, we have selected PROPS1.MLB.

The roll-up menu shows the first background image from this file (you can see more by clicking on the scroll arrows under the name). Page F29 of the ClipArt manual also shows all the images from this file. We shall accept this first file, with the name ALIEN PLANET. Click on the Place button to adopt it into the animation window.

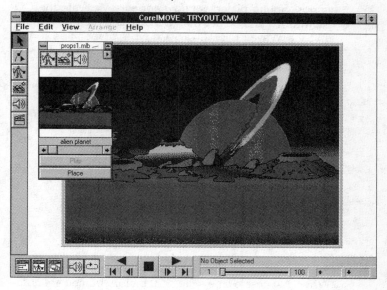

An actor from the laser disk is placed in the animation window in exactly the same way. Select *Open Library* from the Library roll-up menu and select the ALIENS.MLB file from the same directory as previously. Page F2 of the ClipArt manual shows all the images from this file. You can also view them by clicking on the scroll arrows in the roll-up menu. We shall make use of the ALIEN SHIP WAVING image. If the image is not already in motion, by clicking on the Actor button at the top left of the roll-up and then on the Play button, you will be able to get an impression of the movement. Click on

Place to actually place the image in the animation window.

We shall take the sound from the second laser disk in the Corel package. Open the *File* menu and select *Import*. Click on *Sound* in the subsequent submenu. The *Import Sound* dialog window appears. Activate the CD ROM drive and select the \SOUNDS directory. Ensure that the Waves Files (.wav) file type is specified in the List Files of Type box. A list of corresponding files is shown. Choose ALIENSHP.WAV for the animation. Click on OK.

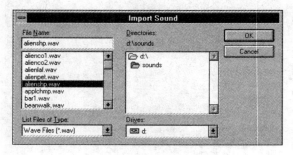

All elements have now been included in the program. When you create a new file, 100 picture frames are automatically made available, as you can see to the right of the slide control on the status bar. When you click on the Play button on the status bar, the slide control shifts towards the right and the film sequence is run on the screen.

9.4 Positioning the actors

The film is not yet a classic. But we shall improve it by getting the spaceship to glide across the screen and eventually land. To do this, select the spaceship and drag it to the left-hand side of the screen. Position it in such a way that only half of it is visible against the background.

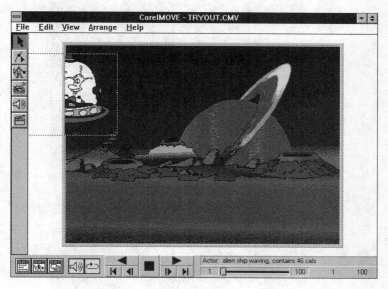

Ensure that the slide control is completely at the beginning. Click on the Path tool to define a route for the actor. A black dot now appears under the spaceship.

Click on the left mouse button once to the right-hand side of this black dot. A new black dot is placed. Keep on doing this until a whole path has been specified for the spaceship (see overleaf).

This will give the effect that the spaceship is landing. Close the *Path Edit* roll-up menu and click on the Play button at the bottom of the screen. When editing the film further, do not forget to move the slide control to the beginning.

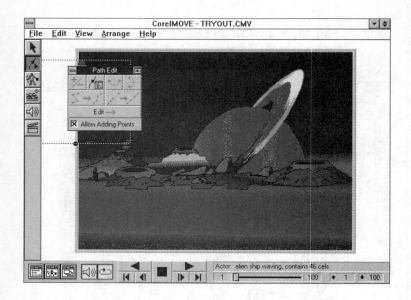

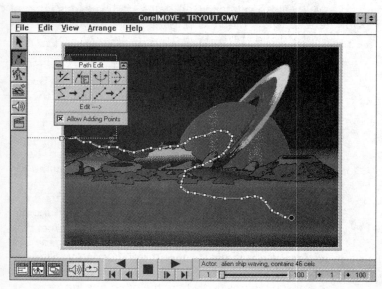

9.5   Subsequent alterations to the film

You should now adjust the background, the actors and
the sound to form a whole. Open the *View* menu and select *Timelines Roll-up*. You can also click on the Timelines button at the bottom of the screen (extreme left).

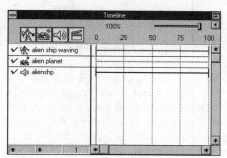

As you see, the actor, the background and the sound
which make up the film are listed. The timelines for each
are shown in differing colours in the right-hand section
of the window. When you place the mouse pointer at the
end of one of these lines, the pointer changes into a
black arrow with a vertical stripe. Drag the end of the
line leftwards. In this way, you can drag the timeline for
the actors for instance to 50, which corresponds to the
50th frame in the film. The actor will then disappear from
the film at the 50th frame. Vice versa, you can have an
actor appear at a specified point.

If you wish you can load a new sound track from the moment that, for example, the spaceship disappears from
view. Ensure that the first sound track stops at the same
moment as the spaceship disappears and load another
sound file which can be played from that moment on-
wards. Open the *File* menu and select *Import* and
Sound. Select, for example, INTRO6.WAV from the
\SOUNDS directory. Shift the timeline so that this file
begins at the position where the other one stops.

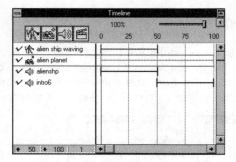

You have now created a short film. You can also pass it on to others who do not have CorelMOVE. To make it available to them you should save it as an AVI file, which is the video standard format under Windows. If the proper AVI operating program is installed, you can run each AVI file under Windows. Consult the Windows manual for more information about this function.

To save a file as an AVI file, proceed as follows:

1) Open the *File* menu and select *Export*.
2) Select *to Movie* in the submenu.
3) Ensure that Video for Windows (*.avi) is shown in the List Files of Type box.
4) Assign an appropriate name to the file and specify the directory in which it is to be stored.
5) Click on OK to actually begin the converting process.

This file can now be played on all computers with Video for Windows. If the film cannot be started from the File Manager, the proper driver will probably still have to be installed.

9.6   Morphing

A morphing program enables one image to blend into another. This can produce fantastic effects, with which you are probably already familiar from sci-fi movies.

The first stage is to open the two images in the program. The transformation takes place in the CorelMOVE bit-map editor.

Open the *File* menu and select *New*. Assign a name to your new file and click on OK. Open the *File* menu again and select *Import*. Click on *Actor from Bitmap File(s)* in the submenu. We shall use two photographs that we have scanned. Specify the required directory and file name. Select the first image.

Click on OK. Now repeat this procedure for the second image. When this image has been loaded, select the image by clicking on the Pick Tool and then on the image. Open the *Edit* menu and copy the image to the Clipboard by means of the *Copy* command.

Drag the second image a little to the side and double click on the first image. The *Actor Information* dialog window appears. Click on the Edit Actor button. This activates the CorelMOVE bitmap editor. As the Toolbox indicates, the editor contains one cel with the actor which has been loaded. Create a second cel by opening the *Edit* menu (move the Toolbox aside if necessary) and selecting *Insert Cels*. Click on OK. The Toolbox now indicates that the current cel is the first of two.

Open the *Edit* menu again and select *Reverse Cels*. A blank cel appears. Open the *Edit* menu and select *Paste*. The second image is loaded into this cel. Now switch back to the first cel via the *Edit* menu, open the *Effects* menu and select *Morph Cel*. The *Morph* dialog window appears. Zoom out if necessary to bring both images into view (activate the Zoom tool, click on the left mouse button to zoom in and the right mouse button to zoom out).

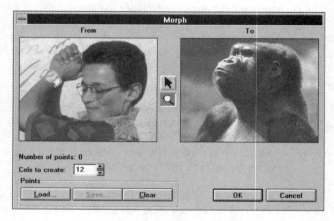

This command will only produce a reasonable result when the images resemble one another to a certain degree. You can also specify certain points which should blend into one another, regardless of the relative positions of the elements of the images. For instance, the eyes of one image are to become the eyes in another. Click on the first point in the first image and then on the corresponding position in the second one. This enables you to control the morphing process fully.

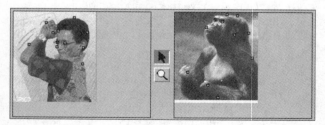

The greater the number of Cels *(Cels to create)* you specify, the greater the number of interim steps that are created. The disadvantage is that the more steps you specify, the longer it takes CorelMOVE to calculate the morphing process. We have specified twelve steps in our example, although more would provide a much more fluent change.

Start the morphing process by clicking on OK. The procedure may take as long as fifteen minutes.

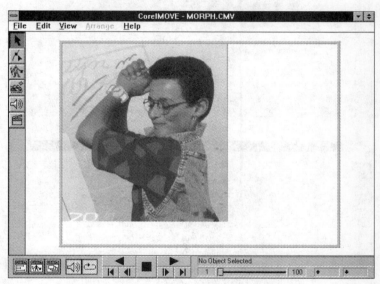

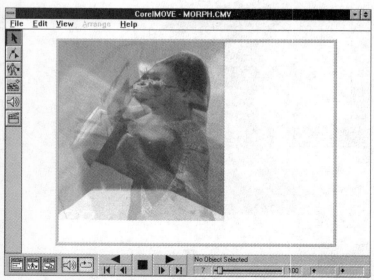

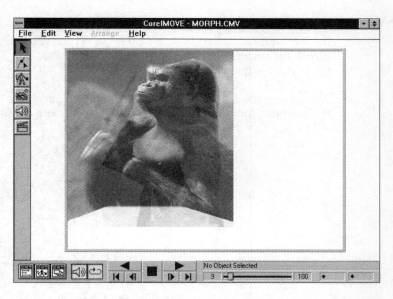

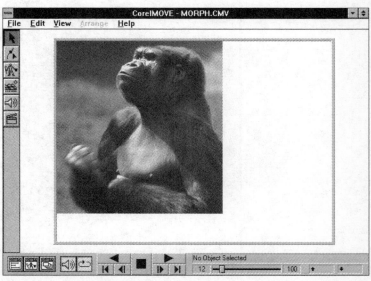

When the morphing process has been completed, open the *File* menu and click on *Apply Changes*. When you return to the original picture, you can click on the Play button to run the transformation.

Just as with the animation film we created, you can save the morphing effect in an AVI file so that other users can also enjoy it on their computers.

10 Desktop publishing with CorelVENTURA

10.1 What is desktop publishing?

The CorelVENTURA program, which is a component of the Corel Package, is the modern version of the Ventura Publisher desktop publishing program. This program enables you to carry out ambitious DTP projects.

In this chapter, we shall discuss the features of desktop publishing and the procedures involved in compiling professional publications. In this, we shall restrict ourselves to a simple example to illustrate the most important principles. In fact, the functionality of the program is very extensive. In addition, the advanced and more professional areas of application will be given a brief outline.

Desktop publishing literally means 'publishing from your own desk', in other words, you use your computer to create documents ready to be printed. Desktop publishing is made up of the following stages:

- entering and editing text
- placing and editing photographs
- editing pictures and diagrams
- editing tables
- combining text, images and tables to form a single document
- designing the publication
- publishing the document.

Using a powerful PC and CorelVENTURA, along with a scanner and a good laser or inkjet printer if possible, you are able to create attractive publications: brochures, folders, magazines, books etc.

While you are running the DTP program, all relevant information is shown on the screen. The WYSIWYG principle (*What You See Is What You Get*) is the basis of creating the document. What you see on the screen corresponds exactly to the printout. Accordingly, any modifications can be directly checked on the screen.

The following list gives an (incomplete) overview of the various DTP application possibilities:

Personal use
- headed letters
- visiting cards
- invitations and congratulations
- preparation of publications such as reports, manuscripts etc.

Company use
- company logos
- forms (invoices, order forms, delivery tickets)
- statistical reports
- press issues
- bulletins

Newspapers, magazines
- dailies
- trade publications
- magazines

Education
- school magazine
- lesson subject matter
- extended essays
- notebooks
- lists

Gastronomy
- menus, wine lists
- visiting cards
- forms

Clubs
- folders and brochures
- agendas
- programmes
- tournament booklets
- invitations

Advertising
- pamphlets, prospectuses etc
- price lists
- advertisements and posters
- logos

Scientific documentation
- manuals, brochures
- dissertations
- synopses.

10.2 Desktop publishing in CorelVENTURA

The function of a DTP program like CorelVENTURA is to combine text, images and tables to form a single, attractive publication. For instance, an advertising folder should consist of text with headings and subheadings, supplemented with illustrations and charts and tables if necessary.

In CorelVENTURA, a document is referred to as a 'publication'. A publication file (with the PUB extension) does not actually contain the texts, images and diagrams, it only manages them. The information is actually stored in various files.

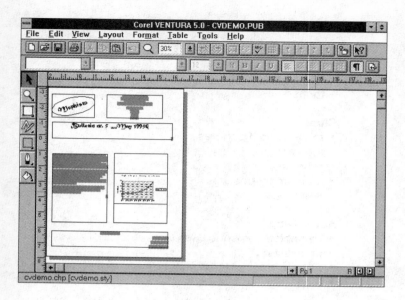

What then is the virtue of CorelVENTURA? After all, we have seen that it is possible to combine text and images in CorelDRAW!. Moreover, experienced computer users know that it is also possible to successfully combine text and images in a word processor like Word for Windows.

It must be noted here that all programs have their own focal point, as it were. It is better to use a word processor for writing text than calculating sums; a spreadsheet program is better for the other way round. Correspondingly, CorelVENTURA is specialised in managing the various tasks, and less suited to elaborating the different aspects of a publication.

A good DTP program is thus a coordinating program for all programs supplying the information. Tables and calculations are made using a spreadsheet such as Excel, images are made using CorelDRAW! and texts are created using Word or Word Perfect for example. Because this information is created using Windows or Windows-compatible applications, you can easily combine the various components in CorelVENTURA. Subsequently, you can make use of the many layout and presentations facilities which, in general, other applications do not provide.

10.3   An example publication

In CorelVENTURA, there are many ways of achieving your aims. Just as in the other Corel applications, you can implement tasks by means of the menu options, the command buttons or the keyboard. In the straightforward example given here, we shall simply mention one option for each instruction, without attempting to give any further opinion concerning the merits of these. You will gradually learn to apply your own preferred method.

Making use of the default settings can also be very convenient. Prior to creating the first publication, you should specify the appearance of the document; in other words, you should create a concept of the page layout. The easiest way of doing this is to take a sheet of lined or squared paper on which you can roughly position the logo, title, text, images etc. This concept will help you in your work with CorelVENTURA.
We shall create a simple folder as an example.

Step 1: Writing the text
The text is normally the greatest information unit in a publication. Although CorelVENTURA does provide its own word processor, it is advisable to use a real word processor for writing a lengthy text. You can use the CorelVENTURA word processor for short texts (see section 10.4.4). We created the following text in Word and saved it under the name CORVTXT1.DOC.

```
Lonely hours devoid of kicks?
Want a mate with whom it clicks?
All the action right on the mat,
Bring a teabag and come down for a chat.
The specialist in
- hardware
- software
- service
- advice
- training
```

When typing the first four lines, press Shift+Enter instead of Enter when you reach the end of each line. Only press Enter at the end of the fourth line. Shift+Enter forces a new line but the text is regarded as being one paragraph. This brings the advantage later in CorelVENTURA that the paragraph text can be allocated the required format in a single action. If you wish to apply different formatting features to the text, you can of course subdivide it into several separate paragraphs.

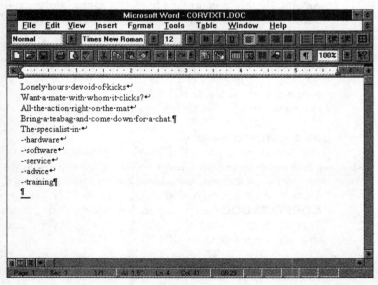

Do not apply any formatting features in Word; we shall create the final layout in CorelVENTURA.

The other texts for our folder are as follows:

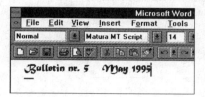

CORVTXT2.DOC

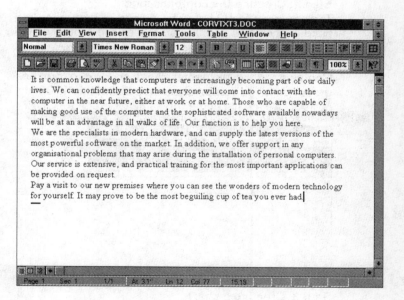

CORVTXT3.DOC

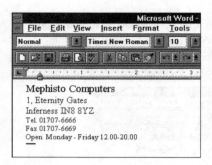

CORVTXT4.DOC

Step 2: Creating the company logo

The company logo should be placed in the upper left-hand corner. You should use the ellipse tool in Corel-DRAW! to create this logo. Switch to CorelDRAW! and draw an ellipse. Place the text 'Mephisto' in the ellipse. Combine the two elements, ellipse and text to form one group (*Arrange* menu, *Combine*) and rotate it 30 degrees. Save the file under the name CORLOGO.CDR.

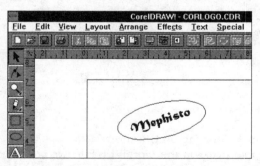

Step 3: Creating a chart

We shall now create a chart to illustrate the turnover in the last few years and the estimated turnover for the near future. This will be shown in the lower right-hand corner of the Mephisto bulletin. You can use the Chart Wizard

in Microsoft Excel to create the chart, or CorelCHART itself. Save the file under the name COREXCL.XLS (if
created in Excel)

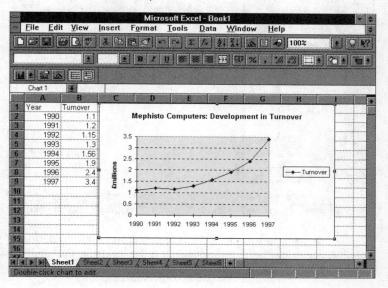

We now have four texts, a logo and a chart. This 'build-
ing-block' principle is extremely suited to working with
CorelVENTURA, since publications in CorelVENTURA
are easily compiled by means of frames on the basic
worksheet of the publication.

Step 4: Starting up CorelVENTURA
Double click on the CorelVENTURA icon in the Corel
group window. The application window appears.

Depending on your own computer settings, the *Quick
Format* roll-up menu may be automatically opened on the
screen. This enables you to quickly select the page format you wish to use. If you do not wish to use the menu,

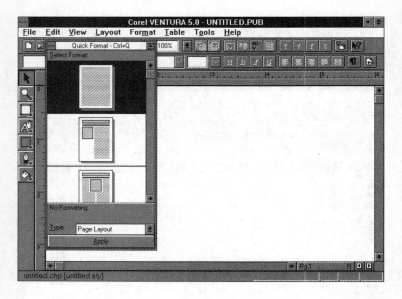

close it by double clicking on the Control Menu button in the upper left-hand corner or roll it up using the small triangle in the upper right-hand corner.

We shall give a brief outline of the first five functions available in the toolbox.

Pick tool
Click on this icon to select elements in the CorelVENTU-RA document area.

Zoom tool
When you click on this tool and hold down the mouse button, a flyout menu is opened. The Zoom to Page function ensures that the entire page is displayed; normally only one fragment is shown at any one time. The Zoom to Actual Size (1:1) button switches you back to the fragment display.

Frame tool
This tool draws frames in the CorelVENTURA document window, in which the units of information are placed (see step 5).

Text tool
This tool is used to type text in the drawing window or to format paragraphs of text.

Rectangle tool
This tool is used to create a rectangle or other geometric figure (see the flyout menu). Do not confuse the rectangle and the frame. Information is placed in a frame, while a rectangle is in itself a unit of information.

Step 5: Creating frames
We shall now create the frames to enclose the information. We begin in the upper left-hand corner where the logo is to be placed.

Switch to the page display. This is done by clicking on the Zoom tool so that the flyout menu opens and then selecting the Zoom to Page tool, third from the right.

Click on the Frame tool and place the mouse pointer on the page. The mouse pointer changes into a right angle. Position this in the upper left-hand corner and drag a frame open until it has gained an appropriate size.

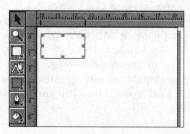

Place the other frames in the same way, so that the page looks something like this:

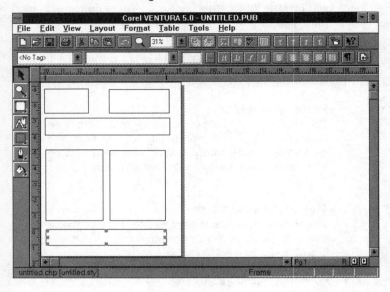

Step 6: Inserting the company logo

We shall now insert the company logo from CorelDRAW! into the frame in the upper left-hand corner. You can do this using a menu command or via the Clipboard. In the latter case, start up CorelDRAW!, open the file and copy the logo to the Clipboard via the *Copy* command from the *Edit* menu. Then switch to CorelVENTURA and copy the contents of the Clipboard to the frame by means of the *Paste* command from the *Edit* menu.

We shall make use of the first method, using a menu command. First activate the relevant frame using the Pick tool. Then open the *File* menu and select *Load Graphic*. The corresponding dialog window appears.

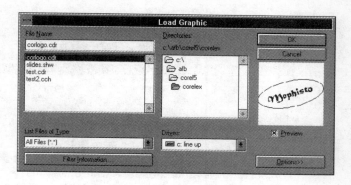

Select the required file from the drive and directory in which you stored it. Click on OK to import it into the first frame.

If by any chance the file is not inserted into the frame, check that the frame is properly selected. Then open the *Tools* menu and select *Files Roll-Up*.

This roll-up menu shows all opened files. Click on the CORLOGO.CDR file and then on the black triangular arrow in the upper right-hand corner. Click on the COR-LOGO.CDR file and then on the *Place in Frame* command, so that the file is inserted into the frame.

If the graphic display appears to be somewhat coarse, open the *View* menu and select *Graphics Resolution*. Then select *High* from the subsequent submenu.

Note: It is advisable to save the new publication each time a file has been adopted. If anything should go wrong, you still have the previous version to fall back on. Do this by opening the *File* menu and selecting *Save As*.

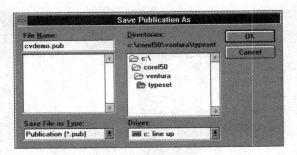

Select a drive and directory where the file is to be stored. We have saved the file under the name CVDEMO. The PUB extension is added automatically.

Now you can save each insertion into the file by selecting the *Save* command from the *File* menu. When a publication file is saved, CorelVENTURA creates additional files (with the extensions CHP and STY among others) in the same directory. We shall return to this topic shortly.

Step 7: Inserting the first text

If you assign a different format to the text in CorelVENTURA, which is a common occurrence, the original text files are also altered. Accordingly, it is important to make a copy of all text files being used and to save them in a different directory. If necessary, you can use these copies without having to fear that something unpleasant might happen to the original files which might make them unusable.

The text from the CORVTXT1.DOC Word file should now be inserted into the frame in the upper right-hand corner. Activate the frame, open the *File* menu and select the *Load Text* option.

The text is imported into the document. Click on the Zoom tool and then on 1:1 to show the text legibly.

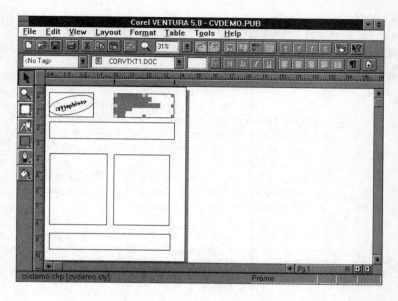

Note: If you wish to remove a frame containing text or an image, activate the frame and press the Del key. The file remains registered in the Files roll-up menu and can be loaded into a different frame if necessary.

The text will have to be adjusted. It has to be fitted into the frame, and we wish to centre it and apply a different font. Just as in word processors, we make a distinction between paragraph and character formatting.

In CorelVENTURA, paragraph formatting has a particularly important function since this determines the total style of the text elements in the publication. In principle, each paragraph can be formatted separately. But in practice, the same formatting is often used for the various paragraphs.

It is advisable to activate the Show/Hide returns button on the text formatting ribbon, so that hard returns and non-printable characters are also shown on the screen. This helps you in structuring the document.

Paragraph formatting is implemented as follows:

1) Click on the Text tool, the icon with the capital A. Select the Freeform Text tool from the flyout menu.
2) Move the mouse pointer to a random position in the paragraph to be formatted and click on the left mouse button.
3) Open the *Format* menu and select *Paragraph*. You can make the required changes in the subsequent dialog window (see the figure below).

You can also save any settings you make, so that you can use them for other paragraphs, or to prevent the Corel-VENTURA default settings undoing them again. Your modifications can be stored in a so-called Style List, in which the CorelVENTURA default paragraph settings are also stored. This list is situated at the extreme left of the text ribbon under the name Tag list (currently showing 'Body Text').

If you have not already done so, click on the Text tool and place the mouse pointer anywhere in the text. Open the

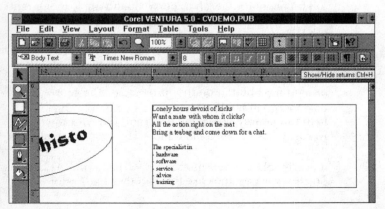

Format menu and select *Paragraph*. The Character tabsheet is active. Specify the font size as 9 points. Click on
OK. Do the same for the second paragraph of text in our
example and specify the font size as 8 points. Now all
the text is shown in the frame.

Now open the *Format* menu, select *Paragraph* and activate the Alignment tabsheet.

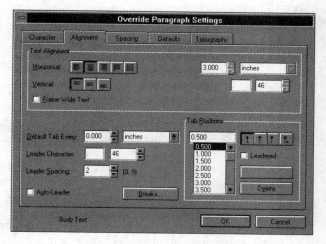

We shall centre both paragraphs. In the Horizontal section, click on the second button from the left and click on
OK.

To make the text more attractive, we select the first letter
of each line by dragging the mouse across it and click
on the Bold button on the text ribbon. The first letter is
now shown in boldface.
In the same way, select the text from 'The specialist...' on-
wards. Click on the Italic button. The text is displayed in
italics.

The text will now look like this (see overleaf):

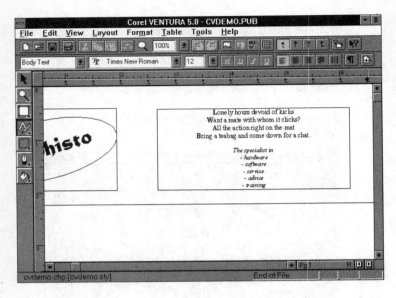

We shall give a simple example of how to adopt a paragraph style into the Tag list. Ensure that the cursor is situated in the appropriate paragraph.

When the changes have been made, open the *Format* menu and select *Manage Overrides*.

Activate the Transfer Overrides To option button and specify a name for the new settings, such as Italics9Centre for example. Click on OK. The style is saved in the Style List in the upper left-hand side of the window. When you type a new text, you can apply this style by placing the cursor in the paragraph, opening the styles list and clicking on the required style.

In this way, you can define various paragraph styles. When you select a paragraph by placing the insertion point in it, the name of the allocated style appears in the Tag List. The details of this particular style can be examined by selecting *Manage Tag List* from the *Format* menu.

The line spacing can be determined by means of the options on the Spacing tabsheet in the *Paragraph Settings* dialog window.

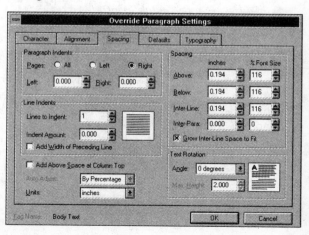

Behind Inter-Line and Inter-Para, specify the required settings for the distances between the lines and the paragraphs respectively. Click on OK to apply the new settings to the text.

In addition, you can also apply separate character formatting. First select the section of text that is to be formatted. For instance, if you wish to apply a different font to the first line, select the line by clicking on the Text tool and drag the mouse pointer across the text. Release the mouse button, open the *Format* menu and select *Selected Text*. The following dialog window appears:

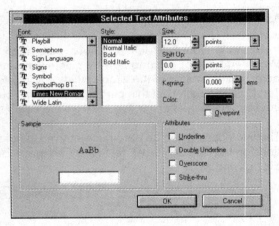

You can now alter the font and font size, apply underlining and change the colour or the kerning (horizontal space reduction between specific pairs of letters, e.g. a capital A and a capital V can be moved closer together). For example, drag the mouse pointer across the text 'The specialist in', open the *Format* menu and select *Selected Text*. Specify a new font for the text, in our example we have chosen Algerian, with the same 8 points size. You can also save this style in the list as described above. The text, enlarged to 200% looks like this:

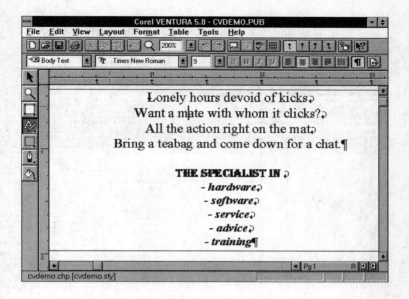

Step 8: Inserting the other texts

We shall now insert the other texts.

Note: If you place a lot of information in a document window, the process of redrawing the screen after alterations have been made is implemented rather slowly. You can reduce the waiting time by selecting the *Draft* option from the *View* menu. Charts and images are then only shown as a cross in the frame. Since they do not need to be drawn every time the screen is moved for example, you can work more quickly. You can activate the *Page Layout* mode again later (*View* menu) to check the progress of the publication.

Activate the third frame using the Pick tool and open the *File* menu. Select *Load Text* as previously and click on the document you created previously CORVTXT2.DOC. If you wish to retain the original layout, use the Clipboard to load the document instead of the *Load Text* command. In our example, we have specified Times New Roman, size 20 points, bold; the text is centred.

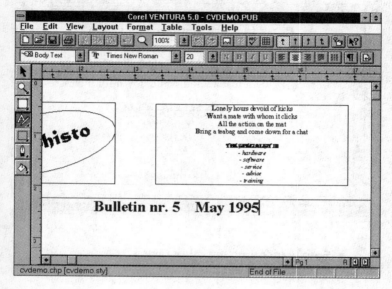

You can save the styles in the well-known manner. When you have entered the text, the publication will look like this:

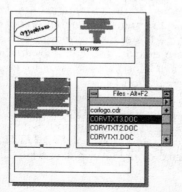

Step 9: Inserting the Excel chart
We shall now insert the chart illustrating the turnover development in the fourth frame. We shall insert it via the Clipboard to demonstrate this method. Switch to the Windows Program Manager and activate the Microsoft Excel application. Open the COREXCL.XLS file and copy the chart to Clipboard using the *Copy* command from the *Edit* menu. Switch back to CorelVENTURA, select the empty frame and select the *Paste* option from the *Edit* menu.

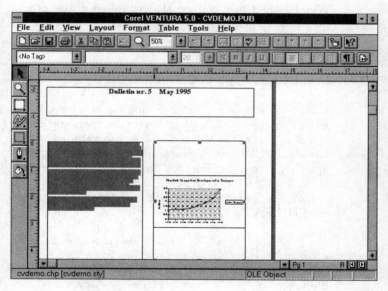

Insert the last text consisting of the name, address, and telephone number of the company into the bottom text box. Apply text formatting features to satisfy your own requirements.

10.4 Special functions in CorelVENTURA

We shall describe a number of advanced CorelVENTU-
RA functions in this section, without aiming to provide a
complete outline of all available features. We shall con-
centrate on those tasks which occur in everyday use.

When actually trying out the information described below, it is advisable to open a new publication each time.
This is done by selecting *New* from the *File* menu.
We shall first give a general description of the procedures used in CorelVENTURA, and the CorelVENTURA
opening screen.

10.4.1 Procedures used in CorelVENTURA

Most programs work with only one file at a time. If you
import an image into a Word file for instance, the image
is then a part of the Word document. In contrast to this,
CorelVENTURA can combine any number of text and image files in one file. The files themselves are not included in the CorelVENTURA file; only the position where
the source file is to be inserted is registered in the CorelVENTURA file.

The features of a publication are also stored separately,
enabling existing text and image files to be also used in
other publications. Changes in these files become visible when the publication is started up again in Corel-
VENTURA.

10.4.2 The opening screen, the menus and the toolbox

The CorelVENTURA opening screen consists of the following components:

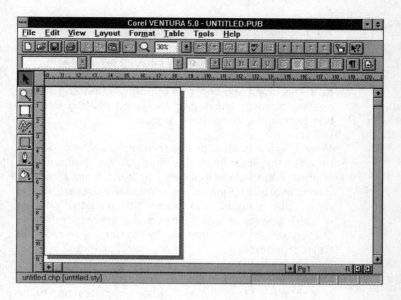

Title bar

The title bar, at the very top of the application window, contains the program title and the name of the currently active publication, in addition to the Control menu button, the Minimize and the Maximize/Restore buttons.

Menu bar

The menu bar is displayed under the title bar. Clicking on the menu name opens the menu. The options provided in the menus enable you to edit and manage the currently active file.

We shall give a brief description of the menus and the options contained.

File: The most important functions in the *File* menu deal with the management of a publication: creating a new publication, opening or saving an existing publication, importing texts and images, and printing the publication.

The publications that were most recently worked on are shown at the bottom of the menu options. You can open one of them directly by simply clicking on the name.

Edit: The *Edit* menu contains options for undoing and repeating actions, copying, cutting and pasting information elements and inserting objects.

View: This menu enables you to switch back and forward between the different display modes. The *Draft* option is important here since it allows you to work more quickly. *Zoom* enlarges specified sections of the document. The other options enable you to switch to a certain chapter or page, display or hide frames and graphics, determine the resolution of the images, and to display or hide the Ruler or toolbox.

Layout: The options in the *Layout* menu manage the various chapters of a publication, style templates, and headers and footers. The guidelines and grid lines are also regulated here.

Format: The options in this menu enable you to format paragraphs and characters, and to design frames, images and tables. The stored paragraph styles are also managed via these Format options, the page numbering can be specified and frames can be anchored if necessary. You can also create a list of contents and an index for voluminous publications.

Table: Tables and modifications to tables are managed via this menu.

Tools: You can activate the roll-up menus via the *Tools* menu. There are roll-up menus for managing the files that make up a publication, for managing the paragraph styles (Tags) etc. In addition, there is a spelling checker, a thesaurus and a function for automatic correction. The

Grid Setup option enables you to position the data elements accurately; *Preferences* deals with the default settings.

Help: This *Help* menu corresponds to the Help menus available in all Windows applications. It can be very useful to work through the *Tutorial* to learn more about the basic concepts of CoreIVENTURA.

The Ribbons

There are two Ribbons under the menu bar. These have various buttons and drop-down lists that enable you to quickly implement functions or select options. These deal with, among other features, managing the publication (opening and saving) and formatting texts (font and font size, paragraph and character formatting).

Not all functions are always available. A button that is displayed in light grey is not available under the current circumstances. If you move the mouse pointer to a button without pressing the mouse button, a small yellow box appears indicating the button name, along with the shortcut key if available. The Status bar also gives a short description of the button function.

Rulers

The Rulers are situated at the left-hand side and above the document window. These help in positioning images or columns etc. in a publication. If the Rulers are not shown, you can display them on the screen by opening the *View* menu and selecting *Rulers*.

Toolbox

The Toolbox is situated at the left-hand side of the screen. The most important tools have been discussed previously. Here is a short summary:

Pick: This tool enables you to select separate elements such as frames etc.

Zoom: The Zoom tool, when clicked, provides six buttons enabling you to enlarge or reduce the display in the document area.

When you click on the icon with the plus sign, you can draw a frame in a chosen section of the publication; this is subsequently displayed enlarged on the screen. The 1:1 icon shows the document in the size in which it will actually be printed.

Frame: The Frame tool creates frames in a publication; you can then load texts and images into these frames. You can also create frames without contents to ensure that certain areas of a publication remain blank.

Text: The Text tool enables you to insert text and to edit (correct or format) existing text. The flyout menu provides two variants:

The text button with the tag has the function of applying existing styles (tags) to selected text.

Rectangle: The Rectangle tool is a drawing instrument. Select the required drawing function from the flyout menu.

If you select the button with the letters AB, you can draw a rectangular text box. Type text in this using the Text tool.

Outline: This tool enables you to modify the outline of selected objects. The corresponding flyout menu contains sixteen functions.

Move the mouse pointer to one of the buttons without actually clicking on it. A small yellow box appears indicating the name of the function. The Status bar provides a brief description of the function.

Fill: When you click on this tool and hold down the mouse button, a flyout menu opens with fourteen different options. These enable you to assign colours and patterns to selected objects.

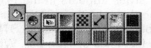

You can change the position of the toolbox by clicking on it and dragging while holding down the Shift key. To move it to another position, click on the title bar of the Toolbox and drag it to the required position. Double clicking on the Toolbox restores it to its original position immediately.

Status bar

The Status bar is situated at the bottom of the screen, and displays information about the publication currently loaded, about selected objects or about commands currently being implemented.

Document area

When the default settings are active, the document area is bounded by the horizontal and vertical Rulers and the horizontal and vertical scroll bars.

10.4.3 Layout

In the example in the previous section, we created the layout ourselves by positioning the frames and placing the various elements in them. However, we can save ourselves a lot of effort by making use of one of the ready-made layouts provided by CorelVENTURA. We can then modify it if necessary to meet our requirements.

To make use of this facility, open the *File* menu and click on *New*. Click on the Load Style button in the subsequent dialog window. The *Open Style Sheet* dialog window appears. Click on the VPSTYLE directory which is a subdirectory of the COREL50\VENTURA directory. A list of available layout styles appears in the File Name box; you can recognise these by their STY extension. If these files are not displayed, ensure that the STY extension is selected in the List Files of Type box. When you select the FLYER.STY style, the document window will resemble the figure opposite.

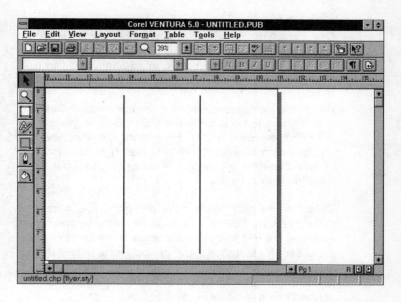

This enables you to directly create a text in three columns that are divided from one another by a vertical line. Examine other styles too. You can also make use of the *Load Style Sheet* option from the *Layout* menu, or the *Quick Format Roll-Up* menu from the *Format* menu.

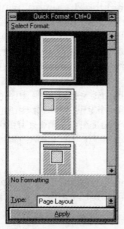

Of course, you can always insert empty frames in a document which you can later fill with information, or leave blank to ensure an open look. In addition, you can also modify the standard templates to suit your own desires.

When you load a new template, the information currently that is going to be used in the publication is given a layout to fit the new template. For instance, if you know that a publication is going to consist mainly of text, you can proceed as follows (instead of according to the instructions in section 10.3).

Create a new publication by opening the *File* menu and selecting *New*. Select a suitable template for the layout and load the text that you have already created in a word processor for instance. Now you only have to create separate frames for images or for smaller deviating texts. If the text contains headers or footers, proceed as described in the relevant section below.

You can adjust the default template as follows:

Adjusting margins and columns
These adjustments are made via the *Frame* command from the *Format* menu. Select the document window using the Pick tool if no frame has yet been drawn and then activate the menu option. The *Frame Settings* dialog window appears. The options on the General tabsheet enable you to determine the size and position of the frames.

You can, for example, specify the exact size and origin of the frame. You can also rotate it and have it recur on other pages. This means that you can place a frame of exactly the same size and at exactly the same position on various pages.

Activate the Margins tabsheet to alter the margins. The options on the Columns tabsheet enable you to alter the columns.

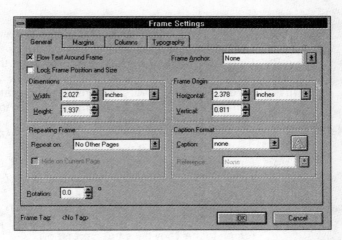

In addition, it may be necessary to adjust the layout within a column in a template, to gain a balanced display in two columns for instance. This is done via the Typography tabsheet.

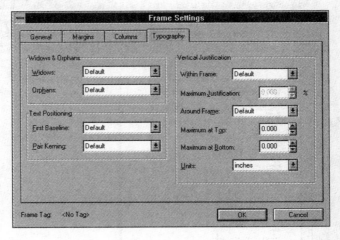

To demonstrate this, we shall describe the steps required to create a layout based on a template.

1) Open the *File* menu and select *New*. Click on the Default Style button.

2) Open the *Quick Format* roll-up menu from the *Format* menu. Select one of the options shown, the third one for example. Click on the Apply button.

3) Activate the top frame by means of the Pick tool and load a text by means of the *Load Text* option from the *File* menu, CORVTXT2.DOC for example from section 10.3. Format the text as required.

4) Load an image in the middle frame, the CORLO-GO.CDR file for example, using the *Load Graphic* command from the *File* menu..

5) Load the text, unformatted, in the column frame. (The columns are not shown but you know from the template that they have been created.).

As you see, the data have been reorganised. The basic text is placed around the central frame.

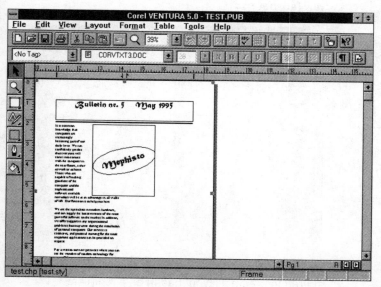

If you modify an existing template to create your own template, you should save it under a new name, otherwise publications which have been created using the original template will be altered when they are loaded.

Paragraph formatting

We have described paragraph formatting in detail previously. Examine the various possibilities available under the *Paragraph* option in the *Format* menu. It can also be very useful to examine the *Manage Tag List* dialog window.

Headers and footers

You can add headers and footers to the pages of a publication by applying a template which provides these, or by defining these yourself. This is done by opening the *Layout* menu and selecting *Chapter Settings*. Select the Header/Footer tabsheet.

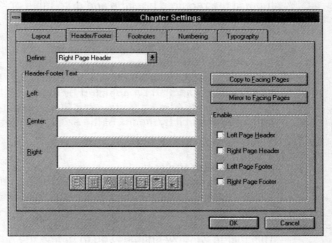

The options on this tabsheet enable you to define different headers and footers for the right- and left-hand pages or for different chapters. The actual header or footer
text is also defined here; you can have it correspond to
the chapter and paragraph titles if you wish.

10.4.4 Working with frames

We discussed working with frames in section 10.3. We
shall give a brief outline of several additional facilities
here.

The function of frames

CorelVENTURA is a frame-oriented program. In other
words, you first place the main text on the basic page in
a basic frame and then supplement it with additional
frames containing images, tables etc. These extra
frames are drawn using the Frame tool. You can place
them at the required position and drag them open until a
suitable size is obtained.

You can also use the *Frame* option from the *Format* men-
u to do this. This method enables you to determine the
size and position with much greater precision. The size
and position can also be adjusted by means of the Pick
tool. Click on the frame and drag it to the required position, or reshape it by means of the sizing handles.

Aligning the frames

The grid points will also help you align the frames with a
certain accuracy. Open the *Tools* menu and select *Grid
Setup*.

This dialog window enables you to define the number of
grid points per unit of measurement (the grid frequency). Activate the *Snap to Grid* option here and also in the

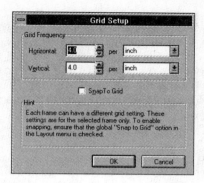

Layout menu. This assigns a kind of 'magnetic' property to the grid lines, ensuring that frames will automatically be attracted to the nearest grid line. Any adjustment in size is also influenced by the gridlines. The grid points are not printed on paper. The *Preferences* option from the *Tools* menu (the Grids option on the View tabsheet there) determines whether or not the grids are displayed on the screen.

These options enable you to align the various frames. Alignment is also possible by means of the *Align* option from the *Tools* menu.

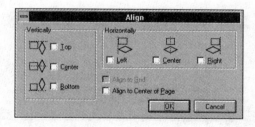

Freeform text
In addition to inserting existing texts, you can also create text in CorelVENTURA, such as headings, subheadings and notes. Activate the Text tool and click on the position

in the frame where the text is to appear. Then type the text.

If you wish to position the text with a degree of accuracy, create a frame using the AB icon from the Rectangle tool. You can format these texts in exactly the same way as imported texts.

Text wrapping

When you place a new frame in a frame filled with text, the existing text is wrapped around the new frame. This facility enables you to insert an image into an existing text.

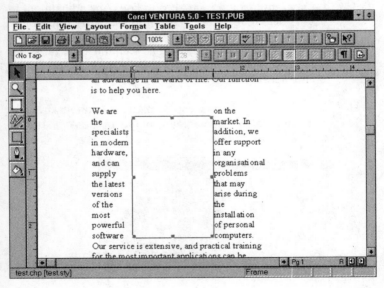

Anchoring frames

You can keep a frame at a fixed position in a text by anchoring it there. Imagine that you have written an article about the turnover development of your firm and you have inserted a chart at the end of the text. Later you decide to add a few words to the article. This means that the chart should also be shifted up to accommodate the new passage of text. Anchoring the frame in relation to the text ensures that this will take place automatically.

This anchoring is only possible in the basic frame, not in frames which have been freely placed. A frame is anchored by assigning a name which appears at an anchor position in the text. Proceed as follows:

1) Use the Pick tool to select the frame which is to be anchored.
2) Open the *Format* menu and select *Frame*. Activate the General tabsheet if necessary.
3) Type a name in the Frame Anchor text box in the upper right-hand section of the dialog window. This name could be A1 for instance.
4) Click on OK.
5) Activate the Text tool and click on the position in the text where the frame is to be anchored.
6) Open the *Edit* menu, select *Insert Special Item* and click on *Frame Anchor* in the submenu. Ensure that the corresponding name (e.g. A1) is shown in the Name box.
7) Click on the option button specifying where the frame is to be positioned. *Fixed to Page* will keep it at one position on the page; the other options anchor it to the text.

If you activate the Show/Hide returns button, all the anchoring positions will be indicated by a small O (the degree symbol).

10.4.5 Inserting lines and backgrounds

Lines and frames

It is advisable to use lines or frames to separate or emphasise separate pieces of information in a document. In CorelVENTURA, you can use a maximum of three lines simultaneously to separate or emphasise these data elements. This is done by means of the *Ruling Lines* option from the *Format* menu. The whole procedure is as follows:

1) Switch to the Page Layout view by selecting this option from the *View* menu. Use the Pick tool to select the frame to which you wish to allocate the extra lines.
2) Open the *Format* menu and select *Ruling Lines*.
3) Select one of the tabsheets, such as Around for example.

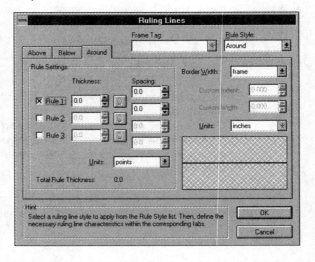

4) Click on the Rule Style drop-down list in the upper right-hand corner of the dialog window. Select

Around from the list. Click on the Rule 1, Rule 2 etc. options to specify the thicknesses of the applied lines.

5)   Click on OK.

Backgrounds
If you wish to allocate a special background to a frame, proceed as follows:

1)   Select the frame to which you wish to allocate the background.
2)   Click on the Fill tool in the toolbox (the bottom button).
3)   Select the Texture Fill icon (second from the right in the upper row) from the flyout menu.
4)   Select a pattern for the frame.

10.4.6 Working with chapters and pages

Chapters
In CorelVENTURA, a publication is subdivided into chapters and chapters are subdivided into pages. Therefore, the smallest publication possible consists of one chapter made up of one page.

The display of a chapter and its corresponding pages is determined by the page layout which in turn is determined by the original layout template stored in a file with the STY extension. You can apply different layout templates to different chapters of a publication. If you wish to assign a different layout to certain pages within a single chapter, you should divide the chapter into different sections.

When you begin a new publication, select a default template with standard settings for the text and page layout, which you can modify if necessary (see section 10.4.3).

Keep in mind, however, that it is **important** to save the modifications under another name, otherwise other publications will be assigned the newly-created layout; this is not always desirable, and is something that you should actively carry out for each individual case rather than passively allow it to happen to all publications.

A new publication initially consists of a single chapter. A new chapter is added as follows:

1) Open the *Layout* menu and select *Add New Chapter*.
2) You must first save your current chapter. The file is automatically given the extension CHP.

A new document window appears for the new chapter. You can now select a new template if required. If you have created several chapters for a publication, you can use the Publication Manager from the *File* menu to organise the chapters.

Pages
The *Insert Pages* option from the *Layout* menu enables you to insert new pages at any required position in a publication. Select *Frame* from the *Format* menu to determine the page layout, such as a new column structure for example.

If you type or import a lengthy text, new pages are automatically added to accommodate the entire text.

10.4.7 Images

You can import images into a publication, or create them yourself by means of the tools available in the CorelVENTURA toolbox. A number of facilities are also provided for editing images.

Editing images

When an image is imported, it is initially adjusted to fit the frame size. If you wish to alter the image in the frame, you can simply alter the frame itself. This is done by dragging the sizing handles or by opening the *Format* menu and selecting *Graphic*. The Graphic tabsheet is automatically activated in the subsequent *Frame Settings* dialog window.

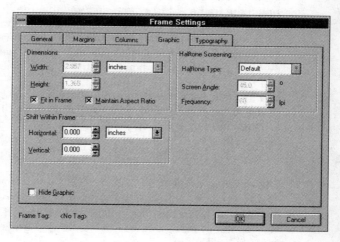

Use the company logo from section 10.3 to try out the various settings provided here. It is sometimes necessary to alter the size of an image within the frame which has to retain its size. You may wish, for instance, to increase the space between the image and the frame border. To do this, proceed as follows:

1) Select the frame containing the image.
2) Open the *Format* menu and select *Frame* or *Graphic*.
3) Select the Margins tabsheet.
4) Type the required values in the Inside Margins section. The preview window shows the effects of these changes directly.

5) Click on OK.

You can use the Shift Within Frame function to move the image within the frame. Specify the appropriate settings in the value boxes.

The check boxes on this tabsheet, Fit to Frame and Maintain Aspect, also influence the display of the image within the frame. Fit to Frame ensures that the image is geared to the frame as much as possible; Maintain Aspect keeps the image as it is, regardless of the size of the frame. Experiment with these settings and with your own images to become familiar with the possibilities.

You can influence the speed with which the screen is redrawn by selecting *Draft* from the *View* menu. Images are then hidden. If you only wish to hide certain images, click on the Hide Graphic check box on the Graphic tabsheet in the *Frame Settings* window.

The drawing tools
The Rectangle tool provides various facilities for drawing shapes. If you use this tool to draw images, it can be very useful to make use of the Rulers and grids (*Tools* menu, *Grid Setup*).

You can use this tool to draw objects in the basic frame in the document window or in a frame that you have selected. In the latter case, you can move, enlarge or reduce the image along with the frame.

The bottom two tools in the toolbox enable you to alter the outline of an object and its filling. These tools are identical to the tools of the same name in CorelDRAW! and are applied in the same manner.

10.4.8 Printing the publication and quitting CorelVENTURA

When you want to print a publication in CorelVENTURA, open the *File* menu and select *Print*.

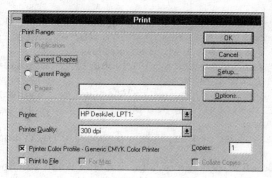

Make the required specifications and click on OK to start the printing process.

To close down the program, open the *File* menu and select *Exit*.

Appendices

A   Installing CorelDRAW! from diskettes

CorelDRAW! has the following system requirements:

- a PC with an 80386 processor or higher and a hard-disk with between 30 and 70 Mb free space
- 8 Mb RAM (16 Mb is advisable)
- Windows, version 3.1 or higher or Windows for Work-groups 3.11
- a monitor supported by Windows, with a vertical resolution of at least 350 pixels (VGA is possible, CGA is not)
- a mouse or drawing board supported by Windows.

CorelDRAW! can only be installed when Windows has been correctly installed. Insert the first diskette from the CorelDRAW! package in drive A: or B:. Then open the *File* menu in the Program Manager and select *Run.* Type the following:

```
a:setup
```

or

```
b:setup
```

You will be asked to choose the type of installation you want. It is useful to select Minimum/Custom here so that you can specify which components of the package you want to install. The full installation is very extensive, occupying a great deal of disk space.

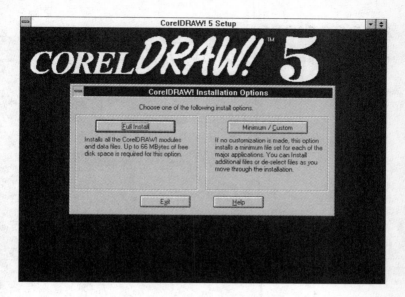

The program recommends that you install CorelDRAW!
in the \COREL50 directory. It is advisable to do so, although you can specify a directory of your choice. You
can then determine by placing a cross in the relevant
check box, whether or not the CorelTRACE, CorelMO-
SAIC, CorelSHOW and CorelVENTURA supplemen-
tary programs are also to be installed. In addition, you
can decide whether the sample files and the symbols libraries are to be installed.

Note: You should only install the symbols libraries if you
have sufficient free disk space. These pictures require
about 6 Mb capacity on the harddisk. You can always install the libraries later, or import a particular one from a
diskette.

When a directory for the temporary files has been specified, a message window appears to indicate that Corel-
DRAW! can be installed. Click on the Install button to actually set the installation in motion.

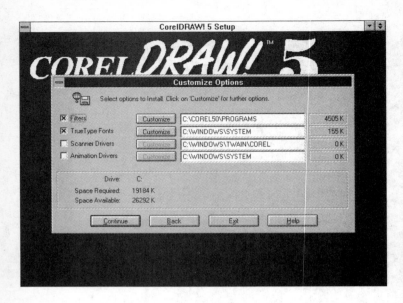

The installation program automatically creates the new Corel5 program group, with icons for the programs which are installed.

CorelDRAW! only supports Windows drivers. Other drivers may cause problems. Consult your dealer if you encounter problems in this field.

CorelDRAW! is started up by double clicking on the CorelDRAW! icon in the Corel5 group window.

Installing CorelDRAW! from the CD ROM

CorelDRAW! can also be supplied on CD ROM. The three laser disks not only contain the same information as the normal diskette version, they also provide a great number of fonts, images (cliparts) and animations.

Installation from the CD ROM is almost identical to that from the diskettes. In fact, the only difference is that you do not have to switch diskettes which means that the process is less time-consuming.

The complete installation will require approximately 65 Mb, but the Minimum/Custom installation enables you to select particular parts of the program, excluding those which are deemed unnecessary.

B   Short guide to Windows

CorelDRAW! only runs under Windows, although Windows is not a part of the CorelDRAW! package. The advantages of running under Windows are evident. Windows represents a user-oriented software concept that has introduced a new way of working with the PC. Windows is in many ways comparable to the Apple Macintosh graphic user interface. The point of departure of both systems is the aim of making working with the computer as simple as possible. Pictures are used to present the available functions instead of lengthy texts, there is a context-oriented help function for each command and it is possible to run several programs simultaneously.

The mouse has become an important attribute in computer use. It has become almost an extension of the arm. Most of the commands in Windows are executed using the mouse (although there are almost always keyboard alternatives). The mouse pointer is moved across the screen by moving the mouse itself on the desktop. When you place the mouse pointer on a name in the menu bar and click, a menu opens.

In Windows and in the Windows-based programs, there are three types of mouse action:

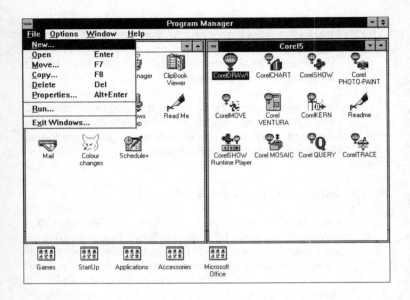

Click

Place the mouse pointer on a screen object such as an icon or a menu command. Press the left mouse button and release it again immediately.

Double click

Place the mouse pointer on an object. Click twice in rapid succession.

Drag

Place the mouse pointer at a certain position on the screen. Press and hold down the left mouse button. Move the mouse pointer to another position on the screen and then release the mouse button. This method is often used to make multiple selections in programs or to move elements.

The graphic user interface

Windows is referred to as a graphic user interface. This means that the screen plays a crucial role in input and output. The interface is the link between the user and the program currently active on the computer. Windows converts the program to a kind of 'picture machine' in which the operating and display elements are graphically represented on the screen. The buttons and switches of this machine are easy to operate and their functions have been standardised. Windows-based programs all have this standardised method of operation, which means that once you have learned how one program works, you know to a large extent how to operate others. For instance, clicking with the mouse in CorelDRAW! has exactly the same effect as in Word Perfect for Windows or Quattro Pro for Windows.

When you have started up Windows by giving the command:

```
c:\>win
```

the Program Manager appears on the screen. This central component of the program functions as a desktop upon which the work is carried out.

When you close the Program Manager, you close down Windows. All other programs can be started up from the Program Manager. All Windows components and applications are displayed in windows that can be enlarged or reduced in size. Accordingly, it is possible to show various programs on the desktop simultaneously which can be very useful in certain situations (comparing, copying etc.).

CorelDRAW! 5

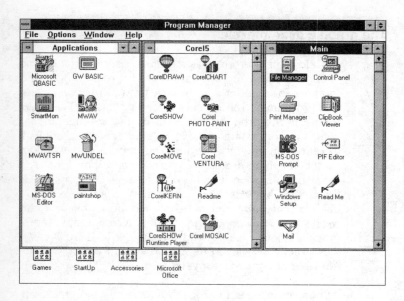

The Program Manager has the initial task of managing the programs. They are gathered into various groups. It is no longer necessary to switch to a certain subdirectory to start up a program. The user only needs to double click on the icon and Windows does the rest.

The figure above shows the three active groups when the *Tile* command from the *Window* menu has been activated. The Main group, supplied with Windows, contains icons representing functions that are important to the way Windows runs. It is also possible to create your own program group under the Program Manager, in which you can include programs of your choice.

To start up a program move the mouse pointer to the corresponding icon and double click on the left mouse button. The program window of the appropriate program subsequently appears on the screen.

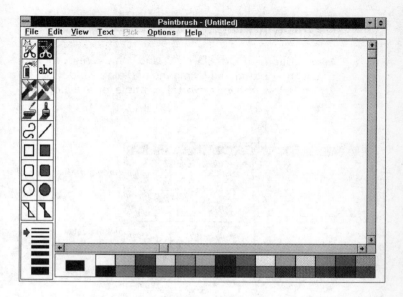

The application (program) windows of all programs running under Windows have the same structure. The title bar is shown at the top of the screen with the menu bar underneath. *File* is normally the name of the first menu, and it contains commands for opening, saving, removing files etc. The last command in this menu is generally *Exit*, which enables you to close down and leave the application. When you click on this command, the application is closed down and you return to the Program Manager.

You will have realised by now that working with Windows is completely different than working behind the DOS prompt.

For more information about working with Windows, it is advisable to acquire the *Windows 3.0 and 3.1* Compact Computer Course in this series.

C Dialog windows

Many options in CorelDRAW! and other Windows programs are determined by means of dialog windows. The figure below shows a typical example of a dialog window:

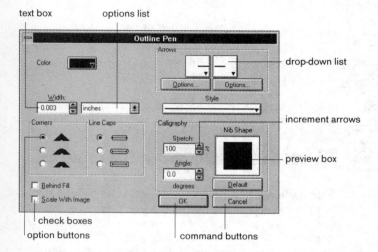

text box
options list
drop-down list
increment arrows
preview box
check boxes
option buttons
command buttons

Operating functions can be specified here.

Option buttons and check boxes
The essential difference between option buttons and check boxes is that option buttons in any one section of a dialog window are mutually exclusive; in other words, when one is activated, the others are not. In contrast, several check boxes can be active simultaneously. Activating and deactivating are carried out by clicking in the box or button.

Command buttons
Command buttons are used to implement functions or commands. Clicking on a command button immediately

executes the function or command. Every dialog window has the OK and the Cancel or the Close command buttons. Clicking on OK activates the specified settings. Cancel enables you to quit the dialog window without activating any new settings. In CorelDRAW! there are other command buttons that you can recognise by means of their (similar) shape.

Text boxes
There are numeric and alphanumeric text boxes in Corel-DRAW!. In the figure shown above, there are only numeric text boxes; these accept only numbers. The text or numbers in text boxes can be altered. Pressing the Home key moves the cursor to the beginning of the text, the End key moves it to the end of the text. Pressing Backspace removes the character to the left of the cursor, or the whole entry if it is highlighted. You can remove certain parts of the entry by marking it using the mouse and then pressing Del or Backspace. It is sometimes possible to change the value in a text box by means of the increment arrows.

Increment arrows
You can change the value of a numeric entry in a text box by clicking on the increment arrows. Clicking on the upper arrow increases the value, clicking on the lower arrow decreases it. When you click on an arrow and hold down the mouse button, the value changes in predefined steps until you release the mouse button.

Drop-down lists
These options enable you to make a choice from various options in a list. Only the currently active option is shown when the list is closed. In the figure shown above, the *inches* setting from the Width section is currently active, but you can change this to *millimeters* for example by opening the list (click on the arrow pointing downwards) and activating this setting. The numeric values change

automatically with a modification in the units of measurement.

Options lists

These are boxes in a dialog window in which a sample is displayed of a certain activated setting. When you change the setting, the graphic display in the sample box also changes to show the newly-activated setting.

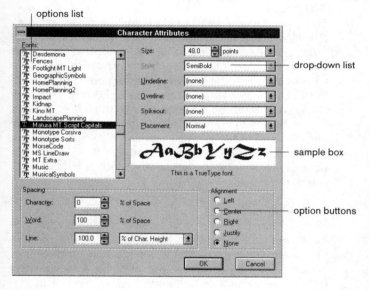

List boxes

List boxes resemble drop-down lists, the difference being that most options are visible. When this is not the case, you can make use of the scroll bars and scroll arrows to move through the list. An option is chosen by double clicking on it.

D   The keyboard layout in CorelDRAW!

The function keys:

F1	Help function - Help overview
Shift+F1	Activate the Help arrow
Ctrl+F1	Activate Search in the Help function
Alt+F1	Activate the Mosaic roll-up menu
F2	Zoom in: enlargement (+)
Shift+F2	Zoom in on selected object
Ctrl+F2	Text roll-up menu
Alt+F2	Dimension roll-up menu
F3	Zoom out: reduction (-)
Ctrl+F3	Layers roll-up menu
Alt+F3	Lens roll-up menu
F4	Zoom in on all objects
Shift+F4	Zoom to page
Alt+F4	Close down CorelDRAW!
F5	Activate Freehand tool for drawing lines
Ctrl+F5	Styles roll-up menu
F6	Activate Rectangle/Square tool
F7	Activate Ellipse/Circle tool
Ctrl+F7	Envelop roll-up menu
Alt+F7	Transform roll-up menu
F8	Activate Artistic Text tool
Shift+F8	Activate Paragraph Text tool
Ctrl+F8	PowerLine roll-up menu
F9	Switch between Full-Screen preview window and normal view
Shift+F9	Switch between Wireframe view and complete view
Ctrl+F9	Contour roll-up menu
F10	Activate Shape tool
Ctrl+F10	Node Edit roll-up menu
Alt+F10	Align text to the baseline
F11	Define the Fountain Fill
Shift+F11	Define the Uniform Fill

Ctrl+F11	Symbols roll-up menu
F12	Specify the object outline
Shift+F12	Specify the outline colour
Ctrl+F12	Object Data roll-up menu

Tab key:

| Tab | Select the next object |
| Shift+Tab | Select the previous object |

Shortcut keys for menu functions

File menu

Ctrl+N	New file
Ctrl+O	Open file
Ctrl+S	Save file
Ctrl+P	Print file

Edit menu

Ctrl+Z	Undo last action
Alt+Enter	Redo last undo
Ctrl+R	Repeat last action
Ctrl+X	Cut from current document to Clipboard
Ctrl+C	Copy from current document to Clipboard
Ctrl+V	Paste from Clipboard
Del	Delete object
Ctrl+D	Duplicate object

View menu

| Ctrl+W | Redraw window |

Layout menu

| Ctrl+Y | Snap to Grid |

Arrange menu

Ctrl+A	Align objects
Shift+PgUp	Place object in the foreground
Shift+PgDn	Place object in the background
Ctrl+PgUp	Move object one level forwards
Ctrl+PgDn	Move object one level backwards
Ctrl+G	Group objects
Ctrl+U	Ungroup objects
Ctrl+L	Combine objects
Ctrl+K	Break apart
Ctrl+Q	Convert to curves

Effects menu

Ctrl+B	Blend roll-up menu
Ctrl+E	Extrude roll-up: add a 3rd dimension

Text menu

Ctrl+T	Character Attributes dialog window
Ctrl+F	Fit text to path
Ctrl+Shift+T	Edit text

Special menu

Ctrl+J	Set preferences

E   Overview of the buttons

Here is a compact overview of the most important graphic facilities. It is a good idea to copy this section and place it next to the computer for easy reference.

CorelDRAW!

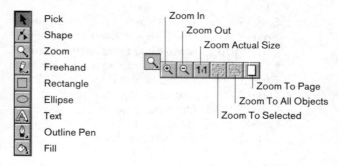

- Pick
- Shape
- Zoom
- Freehand
- Rectangle
- Ellipse
- Text
- Outline Pen
- Fill

Zoom In
Zoom Out
Zoom Actual Size
Zoom To Page
Zoom To All Objects
Zoom To Selected

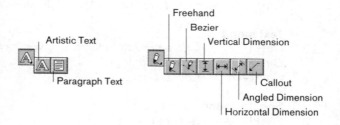

Artistic Text
Paragraph Text

Freehand
Bezier
Vertical Dimension
Callout
Angled Dimension
Horizontal Dimension

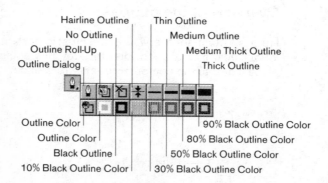

Hairline Outline
No Outline
Outline Roll-Up
Outline Dialog
Thin Outline
Medium Outline
Medium Thick Outline
Thick Outline

Outline Color
Outline Color
Black Outline
10% Black Outline Color
90% Black Outline Color
80% Black Outline Color
50% Black Outline Color
30% Black Outline Color

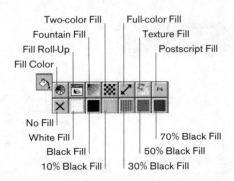

Two-color Fill
Fountain Fill
Fill Roll-Up
Fill Color

Full-color Fill
Texture Fill
Postscript Fill

No Fill
White Fill
Black Fill
10% Black Fill

70% Black Fill
50% Black Fill
30% Black Fill

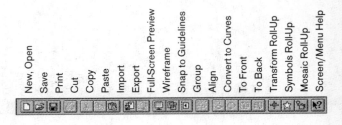

New, Open
Save
Print
Cut
Copy
Paste
Import
Export
Full-Screen Preview
Wireframe
Snap to Guidelines
Group
Align
Convert to Curves
To Front
To Back
Transform Roll-Up
Symbols Roll-Up
Mosaic Roll-Up
Screen/Menu Help

CorelCHART

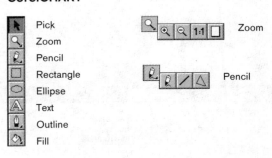

Pick
Zoom
Pencil
Rectangle
Ellipse
Text
Outline
Fill

Zoom

Pencil

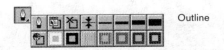

Outline

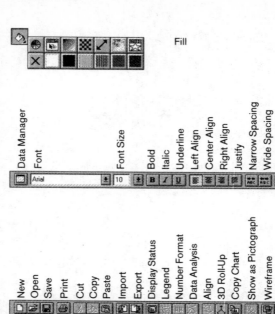

Fill

Chart Worksheet View

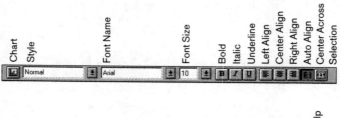

CorelPHOTO-PAINT

Object Picker
Rectangle Mask
Zoom
Eyedropper
Local Undo
Line
Paint Brush
Rectangle
Text
Fill
Smear
Clone

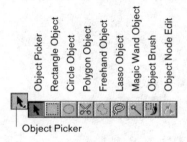

Object Picker
Rectangle Object
Circle Object
Polygon Object
Freehand Object
Lasso Object
Magic Wand Object
Object Brush
Object Node Edit

Object Picker

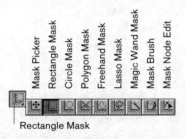

Mask Picker
Rectangle Mask
Circle Mask
Polygon Mask
Freehand Mask
Lasso Mask
Magic Wand Mask
Mask Brush
Mask Node Edit

Rectangle Mask

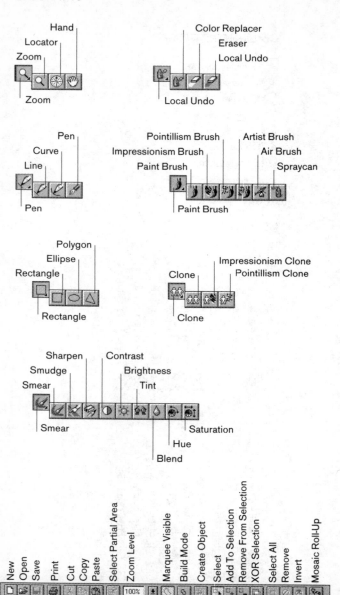

Text Tool active

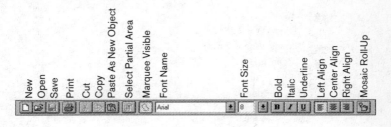

CorelSHOW

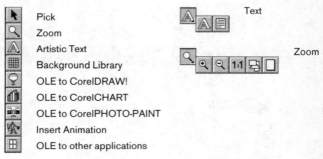

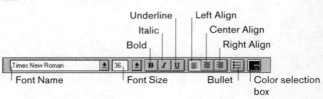

CorelTRACE

Pick	
Magic Wand (Plus)	
Magic Wand (Minus)	
Zoom In	
Zoom Out	
Eyedropper	

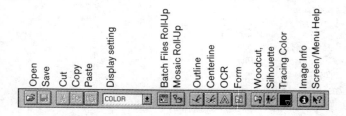

CorelMOVE

Pick	
Path	
Actor	
Prop	
Sound	
Cue	

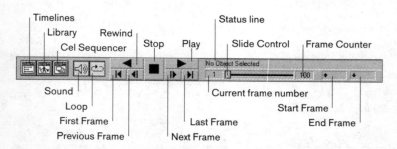

Index

Index